Environmental Law: A Very Short Introduction

VERY SHORT INTRODUCTIONS are for anyone wanting a stimulating and accessible way into a new subject. They are written by experts, and have been translated into more than 45 different languages.

The series began in 1995, and now covers a wide variety of topics in every discipline. The VSI library now contains over 500 volumes—a Very Short Introduction to everything from Psychology and Philosophy of Science to American History and Relativity—and continues to grow in every subject area.

Very Short Introductions available now:

Available soon:

For more information visit our website

www.oup.com/vsi/

Elizabeth Fisher

ENVIRONMENTAL LAW

A Very Short Introduction

OXFORD
UNIVERSITY PRESS

OXFORD
UNIVERSITY PRESS

Great Clarendon Street, Oxford, OX2 6DP,
United Kingdom

Oxford University Press is a department of the University of Oxford.
It furthers the University's objective of excellence in research, scholarship,
and education by publishing worldwide. Oxford is a registered trade mark of
Oxford University Press in the UK and in certain other countries

Published in the United States of America by Oxford University Press
198 Madison Avenue, New York, NY 10016, United States of America

British Library Cataloguing in Publication Data
Data available

Library of Congress Control Number: 2017940855

ISBN 978-0-19-879418-9

Printed and bound by
CPI Group (UK) Ltd, Croydon, CR0 4YY

Contents

Acknowledgements

I am indebted to the many readers who gave their time and thought in commenting on previous drafts of this work. Derek Anderson, Arthur, Corin, and Roderick Bagshaw, Emily Barritt, Sanja Bogojević, Matt Dyson, Michèle Finck, Ronnie Harding, Christopher Marsh, Dhvani Mehta, Jenny Nugee, Pasky Pascual, Brian Preston, Elizabeth Rowe, Eloise Scotford, Sidney Shapiro, Giles Spackman, Kristian Stojanovic, Steven Vaughan, Wendy Wagner, Ceri Warnock, and several OUP reviewers have all made this a far better book than it would have been without their input. Any errors or omissions remain my own.

March 2017

List of illustrations

List of abbreviations

CJEU	Court of Justice of the European Union
COP	Conference of Parties
EEC	European Economic Community
EIA	environmental impact assessment
EPA	Environmental Protection Agency
ESA	Endangered Species Act 1973
GATT	General Agreement on Tariffs and Trade
IPCC	Intergovernmental Panel on Climate Change
NEPA	National Environmental Policy Act 1969
NSWLEC	New South Wales Land and Environment Court
OECD	Organisation for Economic Co-operation and Development
SAC	Special Area of Conservation
SEA	strategic environmental assessment
SPA	Special Protection Area
SPS	Sanitary and Phytosanitary
SSSI	Site of Special Scientific Interest
TFEU	Treaty on the Functioning of the European Union
UNEP	United Nations Environment Programme
UNFCCC	United Nations Framework Convention on Climate Change
WTO	World Trade Organization

Chapter 1
Troubles

Environmental law is the law relating to environmental problems.
This bland sentence conceals much. 'Environmental problems'
encompass myriad troubles to do with our surrounding physical
environment—air pollution, water pollution, land degradation,
species extinction, deforestation, anthropocentric climate
change—the list goes on. All these troubles are collective in
nature. They are caused by the actions of many and they impact
many. These are real troubles. Real in a physical sense, in that
environmental problems are problems because they adversely
impact upon human and ecological health. Water and air
pollution is linked to a series of health problems. Land
degradation results in infertile soils. Anthropocentric climate
change threatens life on the planet.

They are also real troubles in the sense that these environmental
problems confront political communities with a series of questions
that rarely have easy answers. These questions are raised in the
making of decisions. Should a forest be logged? What should be
the pollution emissions from a factory? They are questions
embedded in political programmes and manifestos. What is
acceptable air quality for a city? What types of energy sources
should be allowed and supported by a society? Should the rights
of property owners be limited so as to protect nature? These
questions are also philosophical questions about reason, freedom,

and the nature of a good society. What limits should be placed on individual freedom to protect future generations? What value—ethical, market, or otherwise—should be placed on the natural world? And how do we understand what the natural world is anyway?

Environmental problems are thus the troubles of politics, society, economics, and philosophy. In being so, they are often bitter troubles, revealing deep divisions in societies over how life should be lived. These divisions concern global environmental problems and also environmental issues that affect specific communities. The troubles of environmental problems are also interwoven into the fabric of mainstream political life, as the 2016 US presidential election showed—environmental regulation, particularly in relation to climate change, was a major political issue.

The troubles of law

Environmental problems are also the troubles of law. Environmental law is a necessary response to environmental problems. Necessary in an instrumental sense—legislation, case law, international agreements, and regulatory strategies have all developed to address the collective nature of environmental problems. But law is also necessary in a more fundamental sense. Environmental law ensures that collective action in relation to environmental problems is authoritative and consistent with the rule of law and other principles of legitimate action. As environmental problems need continued management—the steady and even-handed addressing of causes and effects—this is important.

But while environmental law is necessary, the development and operation of it is not straightforward. The troubles of environmental problems do not disappear at the courthouse door, when legislation is passed, or when an international treaty is signed. Law is a distinct field of practice, but in responding to environmental problems it is also responding to social, political, and economic troubles.

Furthermore, environmental law does not have an ancient heritage—a legal lineage in which the explicit development of the subject can be traced over the centuries. Most environmental law was created in the last fifty years. It grew and matured because existing legal systems contained little in them to address the complex collective nature of environmental problems. Environmental law is built on existing legal frameworks, but often requires the development of new legal obligations and doctrine. This not only means the subject is a mixture of the legally conventional and the legally novel, but also that this process is unsettling and requires reflection on what it is possible for law to do, and to be.

Songlines

This book is a *Very Short Introduction* to the substance of environmental law. It won't make you a lawyer, it won't save the world, but it will give you an appreciation for the nuance and difficulties of this area of law. It is a book that maps how interdependent societies across the world develop robust and legitimate bodies of law to address environmental problems.

Maps are not neutral. They are powerful devices. They help us navigate the world, particularly the world of ideas. They tell us what is important and what is not important. They frame how we see the world and what is understood to be important. They shape imaginations and our sense of what is possible. The lines of a map, what it charts and how it charts it, are never preordained.

The choices in plotting and charting environmental law are many. There is not agreement about what is included in the subject. Is chemicals regulation included? Town planning law? Even if there is agreement over subject matter there is divergence of opinion over whether the focus should be on international law or national law or even local government law. There is also the issue of how much emphasis should be given to policy and institutions. Law is often only one part of a multifaceted regime.

There are also many dangers in the mapping process. Given how many environmental laws there are, a map could be a long list of different laws that gives no appreciation for the way in which environmental problems and the struggles around them resonate through the subject. A map could be an act of rationalization, suggesting order when there is none. The legal systems of different countries are also unique (see Chapter 6), and providing a map might suggest a universality to law that does not exist.

The essayist Joshua Jelly-Schapiro describes how maps provide context. In doing so they are often grounded in a love of place, and most importantly 'forge meaning'. The map in this book is thus a map of those things which give meaning and thus sense to this intricate area of legal practice. Many jurisdictions are covered, although primary emphasis is given to those of the English-speaking world.

This book maps the dynamics in developing and maintaining a robust body of environmental law. Mapping those dynamics is akin to charting songlines. Indigenous Australian songlines, made famous by Bruce Chatwin, are tracks across the land that give meaning. The paths of these are recorded in song, but also in dance and painting. Songlines are knowledge systems embedded in cultural practices. They are particularly important because they relate to the coming into existence of the land. The language of songlines highlights the features of many maps—that maps are active ways of interacting with the world. By mapping the songlines of environmental law I am mapping its intellectual highways and byways. These are the analytical pathways that environmental lawyers pass along. They are the tracks that take them in particular directions and on certain trajectories and have symbolic and practical meaning for environmental lawyers. They are the navigational routes of the subject. They have come into being due to the complexity of environmental problems and the legal and political struggles those environmental problems give rise to.

These different songlines intersect and intertwine. My exploration of environmental law tracks back and forth across its vast landscape. There is no linear path through this terrain. My material does not just consist of cases, legislation, treaties, and the work of legal scholars. It also includes the writings of essayists, novelists, anthropologists, sociologists, and political thinkers. Understanding the legal substance of environmental law requires understanding the place of law and the environment in the world.

Chapter 2
Environmental problems

Environmental law is the law relating to environmental problems. The inherent complexity of environmental problems resonates throughout the creation and operation of environmental law. It shapes its structure and gives rise to questions that push the legal imagination of lawyers. It also means that no matter how well crafted an environmental law is, there will always be controversy. Having a grasp of environmental problems is thus a first and important step in grasping environmental law.

Environmental problems come in many shapes and sizes—air pollution in Delhi, wilderness destruction in Australia, waste dumping in Italy—and each of these problems has its own politics and is embedded in a different cultural context. But despite this diversity, environmental problems do have a common structure. To see that structure, let me tell a mundane story from right outside my front door.

The streets of East Oxford

I live in a long narrow street in East Oxford. The houses in the street, like the streets around it, are mostly small Victorian terraced houses with no driveways and no garages. When I first moved in, during the 1990s, there was plenty of parking on the streets in the area. The narrowness of the roads meant that there was not enough room for cars to park on both sides, but this problem had been solved through an informal solution—cars parking half on the pavement and half off it. This reduced these two-way streets to the width of one car but, as there were plenty of parking spaces (and thus passing spaces), that didn't matter. If cars parked considerately, which they did, there was also room on the pavement for pedestrians to pass. Those that lived in the street had pride in their ability to self-regulate parking—we even closed the street on occasion, cleared the cars, and had street parties.

Fast forward a decade and things were different. The number of cars parking in the street had grown in number. There were now very few car parking spaces, and often none. The lack of parking spaces resulted in a lack of passing spaces, and there was often gridlock with two cars meeting and no way for them to get around each other. Drivers would scream profanities. The lack of parking spaces also resulted in illegal parking on corners (see Figure 1). Cars, ambulances, and fire engines found it difficult to access the roads. Cars would often park so far on to the pavement that it was blocked for pedestrians. I, like many others, hesitated before using my car as there were too many occasions when I hadn't been able to find a parking space anywhere in the area on my return. Taxis refused to drop us off outside our front door, stating that once they got into the maze of streets it would be too difficult to get out of them.

There were no more street parties and local residents began to complain to the local authority and the police about the situation. There were petitions, a blog, newspaper articles, letters to councillors, and letters to the local paper. Some of the parking was illegal, but the police did not have the resources to be constantly enforcing parking laws. But even if they had had the resources, illegal parking was only a symptom of a larger problem. There were far fewer spaces than people wanting to park. There was not even one space available per house.

1. Car parking problems in East Oxford before parking controls were introduced.

Tragedies of the commons

Living in the middle of all this was miserable, but the academic in me couldn't help but find it fascinating. The problem of parking in my street was a textbook example of an environmental problem—it is what Garrett Hardin called a 'tragedy of the commons' in a 1968 article in *Science*. The 'tragedy' arises because everyone overuses a public good (in this case parking on a public road) for their own benefit. Hardin described herders overgrazing cattle on open rangeland, but there are many other such tragedies—hunting a species to extinction, depletion of a natural resource, and soil degradation being a few examples. Hardin described air and water pollution as 'reverse' tragedies of the commons. Air and water can assimilate pollution, but only to a certain point. Most environmental problems are such tragedies—they are problems created by too many demands being placed on the finite carrying capacity of the natural environment.

Pondering the parking problem in my street, I was reminded of the fact that it is very easy to transform Hardin's thesis into something simple—a model of rising demand and limited supply—but such abstraction is not helpful. Tragedies of the commons and the mismatch between demand and supply are embedded in societies and intertwined with a range of different social practices. Such tragedies also creep up on those societies. The problem of uncontrolled parking did not appear one morning. There were a few more cars parked in the street every year. When the spaces disappeared, people tended to blame someone else—commuters, people from other streets, and student houses where the six occupants each had a car. People (including me) never thought it was due to their own car.

By the late 2000s, and after local community agitation and a parking survey carried out by the local government authority, the parking problem was finally officially recognized. The relevant local authority proposed a solution—residents' permit parking, with permits limited to two per house. Such schemes are a common technique for managing parking problems and are used across the world. National legislation gave the local authority the legal power to introduce the scheme. The proposal was that in our area cars would continue to park half on the pavement, but in painted bays and with spaces in between so that cars could pass each other.

The local authority consulted the public and it immediately became clear that the proposal was controversial among people in the locality—some saw no parking problem, others didn't want to pay for permits, others didn't want the legalizing of parking on the pavements, others felt it would adversely affect trade in local shops, others wanted more or fewer permits, and others wanted more radical solutions to parking problems. No one thought very much about the fact that the street had a finite capacity for parking places. The focus of the debate was on the right to park, the need to park, and the desire to park.

The issue became a matter of local politics, and threaded through the debate were arguments about the proper role of government and what was a legitimate way to make decisions about parking control. These disagreements were heightened by long-running political divisions in the area and dramatic cuts to local government budgets. The scheme was originally proposed to cover a large area of East Oxford, but after several rounds of consultation, many heated public meetings, and a number of years, a residents' permit scheme was finally introduced in 2012 in only a small subset of streets of those originally proposed.

The finite capacity of the physical environment

The story of parking in East Oxford is a story of many things, but first and foremost it is a story about the finite capacity of the physical environment. Whatever the hopes and expectations there were about parking, the reality was that in the street there were only so many spaces for cars to park. Nothing could change that fact.

Just as with parking in the street, the Earth's environment also has a finite carrying capacity and limited resources. That finite capacity may not be obvious when populations are small and their impacts minimal. But with population growth, industrialization, and urbanization serious environmental problems emerge. Pollution in cities is a prime example of this, but the finite carrying capacity of the Earth's environment is tested in many different ways: through the exhaustion of non-renewable natural resources, the emission of greenhouse gases, the degradation of land and soil, the destruction of wilderness, and by making species extinct. Many governments produce reports detailing the 'state of the environment', which make sobering reading. Thus, the 2016 report for Australia recorded: poor groundwater quality, coral bleaching, water pollution, declines in biodiversity, land clearing, and vulnerabilities due to climate change.

In retrospect, environmental problems appear obvious and the failure to deal with them ludicrous. How can we keep forgetting that resources are limited and pollution is nearly always a problem? Part of the reason is that tragedies of the commons do not have pre-printed labels on them, and such problems are often very hard to identify as problems at all. The finite nature of the Earth's carrying capacity is often invisible, and only appears (and sometimes only in glimpses) through careful scientific study.

Science

Science has played a fundamental role in increasing our understanding of environmental problems. We know far more about the impact of chemicals on the environment and human health than we did a hundred years ago, and the same is true of our understanding of the holistic nature of ecosystems. Scientific practice allows us to understand and record environmental problems and thus is crucial in doing something about them. The comprehensive work done by a multitude of scientists across the world on climate change, and synthesized into reports by the Intergovernmental Panel on Climate Change (IPCC), has made clear the implications of the emission of greenhouse gases. Without that research, action in relation to climate change would not be possible.

But the study of environmental problems is challenging. Research about the environment rarely has the luxury of the controlled environment of the laboratory. Diagnoses of cancer are rising in Western populations, but that rise can be correlated to a range of factors. Some of these factors are environmental, but others relate to lifestyle choices and to an ageing population. Scientific knowledge is also limited by the fact that in studying the environment we are studying large holistic systems in which there are multiple interconnected elements.

The relationships between cause and effect are also delayed. Our emissions today will cause problems in the future and that has implications for our responses. As The Hague District Court in the 2015 *Urgenda* court case concerning the Dutch government's actions in regards to climate change, stated:

> In the words of Urgenda [the litigant bringing the case]: trying to slow down climate change is like trying to slow down an oil tanker that has to shut down its engines hundreds of kilometres off the coast not to hit the quay. If you shut down the engines when the quay is in sight, it is inevitable that the oil tanker will sooner or later hit the quay.

Moreover, the relationship between cause and effect is often non-linear. The second tonne of pollution in a river will have a greater adverse impact that the first tonne. Our understanding of complex ecological systems is also often theoretically incomplete.

Providing an accurate scientific account of the current state of the environment requires the development of scientific methods. Counting bird populations is not an exercise in going into a forest and asking all the birds to line up in a neat row, but rather requires techniques to ensure that observations are as rigorous and accurate as possible. Take the survey of parking in East Oxford. It only recorded one day. Was that a typical day, or were there more or less cars parking that day than on average? And how do you simultaneously measure parking accurately when there are too many streets to monitor at the same time? Studying animal and human populations over time requires serious commitment—personal, financial, and institutional. And some things are easier to observe and record than others. Calculating human deaths from a specific disease is relatively straightforward, but recording mild chronic illness that could also be attributed to other causes is not.

To make matters more complicated, societies are often trying to prevent environmental problems in the future. There may be a robust understanding of a particular physical process such as soil degradation, but assessing whether a distinct agricultural practice in a specific area operating in certain conditions will still lead to soil degradation in ten years is another matter. Understanding climate change is both about making sense of what has happened in the past and forecasting what will happen in the future. Data will always be limited. Our understanding of the physical nature of tragedies of the commons is often as reliable as it can be, but it will never be perfect.

Interconnections

Environmental problems occur in places. Overparking in the streets of East Oxford. Air pollution in the city of Beijing. Deforestation in the Amazon. But as the anthropologist Anna Lowenhaupt Tsing states, 'places are made through their connection with each other, not their isolation'. Environmental problems are the product of a range of different activities that are interconnected. The causes of overparking in East Oxford were numerous—general rises in car ownership, the need for people to commute to their places of work and study, houses of multiple occupation, two-income families, poor public transport to some locations, and social habit. Those causing the problems were not just those who lived in the streets but commuters, traders, and other visitors.

And that is just thinking about a single problem in a few streets of an English city. As the world's economy has grown, the global interconnections involved in environmental problems have multiplied. Supply chains are often long and involve subcontracting across a number of different jurisdictions. These chains have environmental impacts, but ones that are often hidden. The cut flowers I buy from the supermarket do not come with a list of the environmental impacts regarding how they were grown in Kenya and how they were transported from there. Nor is the price of them likely to factor in all those environmental costs, as the price of the product will have been driven by competition in global flower markets and other economic factors.

Take a global issue such as climate change and the number of interests involved, and the causes and consequences multiply exponentially. There is no single group of people 'causing' climate change. Populations across the world are contributing to it, although those who consume more fossil fuels are making more significant contributions. The reasons for those higher emissions are many. Some relate to systemic issues—historic investments in coal-fired electricity production, the lack of public transport infrastructure, how densely populated cities are, and the technological trajectory of car and building design. Other issues relate to personal choice—the decision to drive a bigger car and have a larger and warmer house. Tragedies of the commons don't appear as discrete problems that can be ring-fenced off from the rest of society. They are embedded in social and market practices and it is rarely the case that an environmental problem is directly caused by one isolated factor.

And it is not just that places and environmental problems are interconnected. It is also the fact that a study of a real physical problem—overparking, climate change, water pollution—quickly becomes a study of society and politics. Hardin's commons are social places, political places, places with history, and places in which lives are lived in all their emotional messiness. As the essayist Rebecca Solnit states, writing about a place 'is to acknowledge that phenomena often treated separately—ecology, democracy, culture, storytelling, urban design, individual life histories and collective endeavours—coexist'. Environmental problems are thus problems about how we live together.

Societies, democratic or otherwise, can choose to live in garbage dumps or environmentally degraded suburban sprawl if they wish to. They can choose to make species extinct and to favour natural resource exploitation rather than protecting wilderness. Some of these choices may result in testing the limits of the carrying capacity of the Earth and others may not. Life might be nasty, brutish, and short due to these choices, or life may be less full of beauty, or life may simply accord to someone else's vision of a good society.

14

Values

With that said, most people value the environment. Why they value it varies. One person will value biodiversity as a scientific resource and another because they think every species has an inherent value. Pristine wilderness is beautiful to one person and unattractive to another.

Some of these differences are cultural and shaped by personal geographies. The Australian writer Tim Winton describes how many European settlers perceived Australia as a 'rubbish country' as it was 'so infertile and resistant to Eurocentric notions of beauty'. But having grown up in Australia with the bush on my doorstep, I, like him, find that everything in that country 'is still overborne and underwritten by the seething tumult of nature'. When I started teaching environmental law in the UK I was mystified that the law protected what looked to me like scraggly little fields. I was used to nature conservation being about the battle to save wilderness, but of course there was no such wilderness to be found in the UK.

The divergences of opinion over the value of the environment also reflect deeper philosophical differences. Scholars have mapped environmentalism across a broad spectrum stretching from 'deep green' to 'shallow green' shades. Deep green environmentalism is often described as ecocentric—the environment is valued for its own sake and its protection is viewed as more important than upholding other values. In contrast, shallow green environmentalism is anthropocentric in that the environment is valued because of its utility to humans. Thus, the environment might be protected because we enjoy its beauty, it is important for our health, and/or because we want to ensure natural resources are available in the long term.

These different values will shape how people see the world, and what they think an environmental problem to be and how serious they think it is. For some, the parking problems in East Oxford were about reducing their everyday hassle, while for others it threatened the inherent integrity of the community. A logged forest can be understood as a necessary harvest of wood, or the destruction of something irreplaceable, or plain ugly landscape. The larger the environmental problem, the bigger the divergences. For example, George Marshall describes climate change as 'exceptionally multivalent' and as such 'lends itself to multiple interpretations of causality, timing and impact'.

What an environmental problem is imagined to be will directly relate to what needs to be done about it—whether it requires a radical overhaul of modern society or a series of incremental adjustments to business as usual. Those holding shallow green values are more likely to see current social and economic practices as acceptable, while those whose values are more deep green will argue for more radical options. Thus, some in East Oxford were keen to ban cars entirely, arguing that society needs to rid itself of its car dependence. Others argued that any regulation of parking should not put at risk businesses and jobs in the area, or inconvenience those families who needed multiple vehicles. Any discussion about how to control parking in our area became a discussion about how we should live our lives.

'Good' societies and 'good' government

After the discussion ended and a decision to introduce the controlled parking scheme was made by the local government authority, many people changed their day-to-day practices. Those houses with more than two cars can no longer park the extra cars in the street. The ability of non-residents to park has been severely curbed. Residents are allocated a limited number of visitor parking permits and few short-term parking bays are provided. Commuters can no longer park in the street and park elsewhere, causing problems for other areas. For some this outcome is fair and for others it is not. The decision favoured local residents over other people wanting to park. In doing so it promoted one particular vision about what public streets should be used for—residents' parking—over other visions.

Questions about environmental quality thus are not only questions about values, but also questions about what it means for a society to be 'good'. 'Good' in a prescriptive sense—what societies aspire to and how they expect individuals in them to live their lives and interact with one another. These are questions of the ages and of political philosophy, and as I hope is becoming clear they take on a very distinct complexion in relation to environmental problems. Dealing with environmental problems requires dealing with the patterns of social, political, and economic life. The Indian writer Arundhati Roy sees the building of large-scale hydroelectric dams as a 'government's way of accumulating authority' and a 'guaranteed way of taking a farmer's wisdom away from him'. Naomi Klein notes that the failure to tackle climate change comprehensively is due to the fact that doing so would 'fundamentally conflict with deregulated capitalism'.

The challenges of addressing environmental problems are also at a more prosaic level. Regardless of ideology, the actions of those contributing to environmental problems are often rational, at least from their perspective. That was why Hardin called environmental problems a 'tragedy'—he derived the term from the philosopher Alfred Whitehead's idea of tragedy being in the 'solemnity of the remorseless working of things'. Those parking their cars in East Oxford were not trying to cause a problem. They were just trying to get on with their lives. The grower of the flowers I buy in a supermarket is trying to make a living. The supermarket is trying to make a profit through selling something I want—a profit that is important to their shareholders. And I am buying the flowers as a present to show someone my appreciation. Take any set of common causes of environmental problems and a similar set of patterns emerges. The lack of intent on the part of different actors does not make these problems any less real or serious, but it does make

17

responding to them more challenging. It also explains why societies can simultaneously commit to environmental protection in the abstract, while condoning practices that undercut that commitment.

Questions about a 'good' society become questions about a 'good' state. Hardin's solution to a tragedy of the commons was the need for a strong state to intervene in the situation to 'coerce' citizens to act in ways to protect the commons. This conclusion should not be read too prescriptively. State intervention can take many forms. The work of Elinor Ostrom and others has also shown the potential, in some circumstances, for community-based approaches to managing common-pool resources successfully. What Hardin was really highlighting is that self-regulation is rarely a long-term option for most environmental problems, as the collective nature of tragedies requires some form of coordinated response. The state can provide such a response—it can provide an authoritative account of an environmental problem, it can coordinate needed resources, it can regulate, it can ban, it can authorize, and it can resolve disputes. As we shall see, those responses can take many different forms, but in all cases, to address tragedies of the commons there is a need to limit the behaviour of individuals. That in itself is controversial, and thus a major animating theme in environmental law is the legitimate boundaries of state power in relation to environmental issues.

Chapter 3
The substance of environmental law

Environmental problems have a socio-political aspect, but they are also very real collective action problems that require collective responses. Car parking problems, pollution, and deforestation are examples of where it is difficult for rational individuals to act independently from each other to stop the behaviour causing environmental problems. One person could decide to stop parking their car in our street, but that made little difference and others quickly took that car parking place. One factory can decide to reduce their pollution and increase their production costs, but other factories will not and this will increase the competitive advantage of their products.

Law is the most legitimate and stable medium through which to foster and maintain collective responses to environmental problems. Environmental law has thus developed at all levels of government. It is a dense thicket of legislation, delegated legislation, treaties, policies, regulatory strategies, and case law shaped by the complexities of many different environmental problems. As a subject of relatively recent vintage, it is a mixture of the legally conventional and the legally innovative. It is also operating in highly politicized contexts. To really understand the subject, an understanding of the nature of environmental law is needed.

Diversity

Environmental law comes into existence in response to specific environmental problems, and as the expression of political commitments to address those problems. It exists in many jurisdictions and at all levels of government. It is: the local government laws of sewage treatment in India; the state laws of planning in Australia; the national air quality laws in the US; the supranational emission trading scheme in the EU (European Union); the international treaty concerning biodiversity; and it is much else as well.

As these examples suggest, environmental law is diverse. It is so in three different ways. First, while there are some exceptions, the environmental law of one jurisdiction is not directly legally related to environmental law in another jurisdiction. National legal systems do not exist in a hierarchy with international law. It is not a higher law that always binds nations because it is international. In federal national systems, a federal government may have such power over the states of that federation but usually only within the competence given to them by the relevant constitution. For example, there is a vast array of different local and national climate change laws, some of which directly relate to international regimes, and many that do not.

It is true that environmental law concepts are transplanted between legal systems, but the same environmental law concept will take on a different legal life in a different legal order. Societies and their legal and political cultures are also distinctive. Public law litigation is common in the US, but not in Singapore. Natural resource development is a significant feature of the Australian economy, but not that of Belgium. India and China have rapidly growing economies, but Italy does not.

Second, the diversity of environmental law is a product of the diversity of environmental problems. Each tragedy of the commons has its own specific pathology. The dumping of waste in Northern Ireland has a different socio-political context from the logging of forests in Tasmania. The scientific uncertainties involved in modelling future anthropocentric climate change are distinct from assessing the human health risks from certain chemicals. Addressing climate change requires making decisions about energy use while issues to do with pesticide control interrelate with agricultural practices.

Third, there are a range of different legal responses to tragedies of the commons. Hardin recognized the importance of state regulation (as well as encouraging a change in morality), but the state can regulate in many different ways. It can make certain harmful activities a criminal offence, it can require authorization for an activity, it can set standards for environmental quality, it can regulate technology so as to ensure the environment is protected. Moreover, the role of the state can be less centre stage. Commons can be transformed into private property as a way of addressing tragedies. The EU emission trading scheme is an example of this (Chapter 8). Carbon emissions are essentially privatized and unitized. Individual agreements, upheld by the law, can also be a response to environmental problems. In critiquing a reductionist interpretation of Hardin's work, Ostrom noted that 'many solutions exist to cope with many different problems' arising from tragedies of the commons.

Given all this, environmental law is made up of many things. It includes multilateral international treaties that create frameworks for collective action. The United Nations Framework Convention on Climate Change (UNFCCC) and the United Nations Convention on Biodiversity are two examples of such frameworks. At the national level, there is legislation that requires authorization for polluting activities. The very dry-sounding Environmental Permitting (England and Wales) Regulations 2010 is a case in point. There are also intricate regulatory regimes that create processes for setting environmental standards. The EU Water

Framework Directive does exactly that. Environmental law also includes many court judgments in which precedents are set, environmental disputes are resolved, and environmental legislation is interpreted. There are also areas of environmental law that are more akin to policy than law. The Australian National Strategy on Ecological Sustainable Development and the National Planning Policy Framework in England are good illustrations. Environmental law also includes regulatory strategies and market instruments such as the EU emission trading scheme and landfill taxes.

The vastness of environmental law and the diversity of subject matter means that environmental law scholars often agonize over how to define the subject and what to include in it. It also means that most environmental lawyers specialize in specific areas. International environmental lawyers thus share little of the expertise of national environmental lawyers, and in each of these fields scholars and lawyers usually focus on specific subject areas. Just as you wouldn't ask for medical advice from a dermatologist about your dental cavities, you would not ask a US endangered species legislation expert about the workings of EU water quality legislation.

Material

The diversity of environmental law also means that environmental law does not have a set legal form. It is an amalgamation of different legal rules, principles, processes, obligations, rights, and institutions. It is not like a field such as trusts law, where a lawyer or scholar gains expertise in a particular legal device (a trust). Environmental lawyers are applying and adapting a range of legal concepts to environmental problems.

Moreover, Western legal systems have historically focused on the rights of individuals and the power of states, not on environmental protection. Criminal law developed to define and punish actions between individuals that were deemed to be 'crimes'.

Constitutional law developed as a prescriptive 'power map' of the state. Contract law developed to enforce obligations between individuals. The list goes on. Around these rights and powers developed labyrinthine doctrines, laws, principles, and institutions, none of which had as its primary focus environmental protection. The environment also had no legal identity within these areas of law. Given this, environmental law had to be created. The history of that creative development is charted in Chapter 4, but here it is important to note the legal materials involved in that development.

Most significantly, the majority of environmental law is in the form of legislation. As environmental problems emerged, individual court decisions did little to address them, as courts could only deal with the issues before them in light of existing law. In contrast, legislatures could pass statutes that created a framework for a more comprehensive approach. Thus, in the US there is a suite of statutes—the Clean Air Act, the Clean Water Act, the Endangered Species Act, the Federal Insecticide, Fungicide, and Rodenticide Act, the National Environmental Policy Act, the Safe Drinking Water Act, the Comprehensive Environmental Response, Compensation, and Liability Act, and the Toxic Substances Control Act to name a few. These have been passed at different times and many have also been subsequently amended. A similar pattern can be seen in most other jurisdictions.

While the bulk of environmental law is legislation, other forms of law have an important role to play. Legislation is often accompanied by policies, regulatory strategies, and other non-legal devices that have legal implications. Regulatory strategies (Chapter 8) are examples of attempts to refashion law to make it more effective in addressing environmental problems. At the international level, there exist international treaties, conventions, and other forms of international agreements that address environmental problems. International law is the law of consenting states, and thus the 'binding' nature of these laws is not straightforward (Chapter 5).

While courts are limited in providing initial responses to environmental problems, they play a fundamental role in interpreting and applying legislation. They also adjudicate on the many disputes that arise in relation to environmental problems. To do that they must consider the legal arguments of the parties to a dispute, 'stabilize the facts' (usually with the aid of rules of evidence), and authoritatively rule on the outcome of a case and provide a reasoned judgment for that ruling. While rates of litigation vary between countries, this role of the court is not uncommon. As the American legal scholar Karl Llewellyn noted, 'our society is honeycombed with disputes', and that is particularly true when it comes to environmental problems.

The pursuit of stability

Describing the materials of environmental law does not impart the internal dynamics of the subject or provide evidence of its animating songlines. In particular, it gives no feeling for a major preoccupation of lawyers and legal scholars—legal stability. Stable does not mean static. The law evolves, whether through legislation or case law, but it does so carefully, guided by a belief in the rule of law. The rule of law comes in many versions and political hues, but overall it is a commitment to law being as knowable as is consistent with achieving the law's other goals. As the philosopher Jeremy Waldron states:

> Since law's presence in people's lives tends to be intrusive if not coercive, it is important that its presence be made calculable, so that it can enter into their planning. And since other people's actions may also impact intrusively upon us, we need to know in advance how, and to what extent, these too will be controlled by law.

Much of this stability comes from the substantive reasoning of law, which is required to show rigour, logic, attention to detail, and be grounded in established principles and doctrines.

It also comes from having recognized sources of law and the need to relate any legal argument to existing laws. As the French thinker Bruno Latour states, 'law has a homeostatic quality which is produced by the obligation to keep the fragile tissue of rules and texts intact'. It is thus very different from science. 'Science can draw on lively controversy but the law has to restore an equilibrium', Latour notes. As such, 'Although one might speak admiringly of "revolutionary science", "revolutionary laws" have always been as terrifying as courts with emergency powers.'

Court cases—the application of the law to a specific set of facts—are important ways of ensuring legal stability. Putting legal arguments to a court is an act in showing how an argument is consistent with the well-established rules and principles of a legal system. Great advocacy and great judging is grounded in knowing and understanding the law, legal reasoning, and the logic behind that reasoning.

The stability of law is also reflected in the way that legal systems have tended to develop around a set of legal ideas and concepts. Contract law is a good example of this. Two parties come together to make an agreement. They agree on the terms, they make their bargain, some form of payment (what is called consideration) is exchanged to seal the bargain, and the law will then uphold the contract. Thus, in England there is centuries of case law fleshing out this basic framework. While there are exceptions, generally speaking, only those who are parties to the contract can enforce it. There are doctrines relating to when the law will not enforce a contractual obligation due to a misrepresentation or mistake. There is case law concerning what type of remedies a breach of contract will give rise to. The law is detailed, but at its core is an assumption that the parties and their obligations are easily identifiable. There are always exceptions to the doctrines dealing with particular circumstances (what happens if Herman gets Frank drunk so that Frank enters into a contract with Herman to sign away his house for a penny), but the presumption is that such problems are manageable through the development of specific doctrines for specific circumstances.

Environmental problems do not fit easily into these existing legal frameworks. There are many interconnected parties. Pollution transcends jurisdictional and property boundaries. There are no generic legal obligations not to destroy the natural world or endanger a species. Many contemporary environmental laws, like other areas of regulation, regulate activities before they become serious problems. This is in contrast to other areas of law that are concerned with the legal implications of past behaviour. As environmental problems are dynamic, laws in relation to them often need to be revised.

This of course explains why so much environmental law is legislation, and herein lies a fundamental dynamic of the subject. Legislation is law, but does not always sit easily with ideas of legal stability and, particularly in common law systems, it tends to be viewed by lawyers as having a second-class legal status. As Waldron notes: 'a statute thrusts itself before us as a low-bred parvenu, all surface and no depth, all power and no heritage, as arbitrary in provenance as the temporary coalescence of a parliamentary or congressional majority.' Waldron rightly challenges this assumption and argues that legislation is 'a respectable source of law'.

Whatever the case in other fields of law, in the environmental law sphere, legislation is not all surface, it is not all power, and it is not a temporary coalescence. Around an environmental statute develops a complex body of law and practice concerning how to apply it legitimately. While environmental legislation can disrupt the legal order by creating new legal obligations, the legal order develops to adapt to such disruption and to create a new stable legal equilibrium.

Legal categorization

These disruptive processes are explored in the rest of this book.
They take many forms. Each process is a series of internal legal
dynamics—dynamics that counter-intuitively ensure legal stability.
It will be useful to examine an example of those dynamics before
proceeding further, as they are easy to overlook.

As environmental problems usually have no initial legal status in
legal cultures, a major feature of environmental legislation is that
it creates new legal categories. If something is in that category, it
has legal implications. For example, pollution legislation defines
what 'pollution' is. If an emission falls into that definitional category,
then that emission may require a regulatory permit and/or lead
to prosecution for a criminal offence. The legislation is disruptive
because no such legal category existed before the legislation was
passed, but once it is passed it gives rise to a range of different
legal questions, particularly in relation to how categories are
legally defined.

A good example of this can be seen in relation to nature
conservation. A common technique in nature conservation/
landscape protection is to grant protection to an area of land by
giving it a legal designation. In England there are at least four
different designations, including local nature reserves, national
nature reserves, Sites of Special Scientific Interest (SSSIs),
and national parks. Each of these designations is for a different
purpose. National nature reserves are for land 'managed for
a conservation purpose' (Figure 2). Local nature reserves are
designated in the 'interests of the locality'. SSSIs are designated
when Natural England 'are of the opinion that any area of land is
of special interest by reason of any of its flora, fauna, or geological
or physiographical features'. These categories overlap, and one
area might be subject to more than one designation. These are not
the only ways in which land can be protected through designation.

2. Sign for Aston Rowant National Nature Reserve. Note the map outlining the area including in the reserve.

Alongside them are Special Areas of Conservation (SACs) and Special Protection Areas (SPAs), enclaves under the EU Habitats Directive and Wild Bird Directives respectively, as well as landscape being designated an 'area of outstanding national beauty' or being granted World Heritage status under the World Heritage Convention

Each designation scheme brings with it distinct duties and obligations. Landowners of SSSIs must seek consent for any operations they carry out on that site. It is also an offence to 'intentionally or recklessly' destroy or damage 'any of the flora, fauna, or geological or physiographical features by reason of which a site of special scientific interest is of special interest'. In contrast, for SPAs and SACs:

> any plan or project not directly connected with or necessary to the management of the site but likely to have a significant effect thereon, either individually or in combination with other plans or projects, shall be subject to appropriate assessment of its implications for the site in view of the site's conservation objectives.

These are two very different sets of legal obligations with two very different sets of operational parameters. 'Operation' is not the same as 'plan or project'. SPAs and SACs require an 'appropriate assessment' in certain circumstances, but the consent in regards to SSSIs does not.

Even the same term can mean different things in different jurisdictions. Take 'national park'. In England, areas are designated national parks by reason of 'their natural beauty' and 'the opportunities they afford for open-air recreation, having regard both to their character and to their position in relation to centres of population'. But in the Australian state of New South Wales, the relevant legislation tautologically defines national park as 'lands reserved as a national park under this Act'. In the US, the legal framework focuses on the national park system made up of different areas, which, although 'distinct in character, are united through their interrelated purposes and resources into one national park system as cumulative expressions of a single national heritage'.

From disruption to stability

These legal categories are being applied and maintained over time. Declaring an area of land a 'national park' or 'SSSI' is the start of a legal process. There are also many dimensions to interpreting and applying these legal categories. For example, the rapidly changing nature of our scientific knowledge about the health effects from pollutants means that in setting primary national ambient air quality standards under the Clean Air Act in the US, there needs to be an ongoing scientific re-evaluation of what are the quantitative standards that 'allowing an adequate margin of safety, are requisite to protect the public health'. Such standards are inevitably controversial. If they are set too low they will fail to protect the health of the population, and in particular vulnerable populations such as children and asthmatics. If they are set too high, they will not be practically achievable and may affect the viability of business.

Or take waste law in the EU. The EU Waste Directive is designed to prevent the production of waste. Reuse of waste is encouraged. If waste cannot be prevented it should be recycled, or disposed of as close to where it was produced as possible. If something is 'waste', then the holder of the waste is subject to a set of strict legal obligations to ensure they are responsible for it. That responsibility is fundamental to ensuring waste is managed properly, but is perceived by industry as costly in terms of time, organization, and resources.

The directive defines waste to mean 'any substance or object which the holder discards or intends or is required to discard' and the application of that, and earlier legislative formulations of the definition, has been fraught. Is burning wood chips, claiming you are using them for energy, really discarding them? Is using pig manure as fertilizer an excellent example of reusing it, or just a loophole through which pig farmers can discard their waste?

Much of the challenge comes from the fact that what is 'waste' is directly linked to something being discarded. As Lord Justice Carnwath (as he then was) noted in one case:

> [t]he subjective 'intention to discard' may be a useful guide to the status of the material in the hands of the original producer. However, it is hard to apply to the status of the material in the hands of someone who buys it for recycling or reprocessing; or who puts it to some other valuable use. In no ordinary sense is such a person 'discarding' or 'getting rid of' the material. His intention is precisely the opposite.

But the ambiguities also come from outside the law. Those being regulated have strong economic incentives to argue something is not waste. Pig manure is a legitimate fertilizer, but only if it is not overused, but overuse is hard to determine. Burning wood chips is a heat source, but also a great way to discard something. The legal definition of waste is revisited with every new factual circumstance.

Examples of legal disputes concerning whether something falls into a particular legal category as set out in environmental legislation thus abound. The courts play an important role in resolving these disputes, which are nearly always a mixture of legal interpretation and the application of the law to the facts. They also occur in circumstances where there are practical consequences. Falling into a legal category will usually result in activities being regulated, while falling outside it means they will not.

Thus, the issue in the US Supreme Court case of *Massachusetts v Environmental Protection Agency* (2007) was whether greenhouse gases amounted to 'pollutants' for the purposes of a provision of the US Clean Air Act, which empowered the Environmental Protection Agency (EPA) to regulate emissions of air pollutants from new motor vehicles. The Clean Air Act defines 'air pollutant' to include 'any air pollution agent or combination of such agents, including any physical, chemical, biological, radioactive...substance or matter which is emitted into or otherwise enters the ambient air'. The EPA, at that time overseen by the George W. Bush administration, argued that carbon dioxide emissions did not fall into that definition.

The majority of judges in the Supreme Court disagreed: 'On its face, the definition embraces all airborne compounds of whatever stripe, and underscores that intent through the repeated use of the word "any."... The statute is unambiguous.' In contrast, Justice Scalia dissented, focusing on the ambiguity of the word 'including' in the definition:

> In short, the word 'including' does not require the Court's (or the petitioners') result. It is perfectly reasonable to view the definition of 'air pollutant' in its entirety: An air pollutant *can* be 'any physical, chemical,...substance or matter which is emitted into or otherwise enters the ambient air,' but only if it retains the general characteristic of being an 'air pollution agent or combination of such agents.' This is precisely the conclusion EPA reached.

The careful attention to the legislative text can be seen in both judgments. There was a clear political dimension to this case, but for the court it raised legal issues. David Markell and J. B. Ruhl, US environmental lawyers, described the case as raising a question of 'vanilla statutory interpretation'.

Legal ambiguity is not only a feature of environmental law; it is an aspect of all law. It is the reason why lawyers start sentences with 'it all depends', and that intelligent lawyers can disagree about the legal implications of a law. The complexities of environmental problems do contribute to those ambiguities, but ambiguity does not mean illegitimacy. Nor does it mean instability. What can be seen is that environmental legislation does not exist in splendid isolation. Around each statute develops a complex body of law and practice that ensures the stability of the legal order.

The substantive nature of environmental law

That body of law means that environmental law is not a passing political fashion, easily shed as the ideological seasons change. Environmental legislation is the product of political legislatures, but it is responding to real problems, and while environmental legislation may be amended, it is constantly being integrated into the legal order. The density of environmental law—its thick, substantive, and non-accessible nature—is a product of this process of integration. Environmental law is a product of the complexity of environmental problems, and the need to adapt the legal order to respond to those problems. This point is not just of academic interest, but is fundamental to a proper understanding of environmental law—although it also has a political dimension, a focus on the politics of environmental law leads to a misunderstanding of what environmental law is and what it can do.

That misunderstanding is often well meaning. People turn to the law in frustration and with hopes of truth and justice. Faced with the scientific and socio-political complexity of environmental problems, law appears to be an answer. Thus, those who are keen to protect the environment often perceive environmental law in instrumental terms—seeing an international treaty, legislation, or a court case as a simple solution to environmental problems. They do not see how environmental legislation gives rise to a new field of legal practice, and that the maintenance of environmental quality requires the steady and legitimate application of environmental law over time.

But this misunderstanding is problematic in another way, as it allows for environmental law to be understood as just politics. Take, for example, the attention that a conference I helped organize in 2015 garnered. The conference brought judges, scholars, and practitioners together from across the world to discuss the legal implications of climate change for adjudication. This is an issue of practical importance—between 2010 and 2015 there had been over 500 cases in which climate change was legally relevant. This is not surprising. Many countries have passed legislation addressing climate change and it is beginning to have environmental consequences, particularly in relation to sea level rise. In all these cases judges were considering legal questions and resolving legal disputes. The focus of the conference was on legal detail, and ideas of legal stability and legal integrity, in a range of different legal contexts.

The conference caught the attention of a small handful of opinion and blog writers, all of whom were doubtful of the science of climate change. They perceived the conference as a political exercise and something akin to ideological activism, rather than what it was—a discussion focused on legal detail. Given the conference topic, this polemical response is not surprising. As the Indian writer Amitav Ghosh notes, disagreements about climate change are 'clustered along a fault line of extreme political polarisation'. What is less obvious, and thus more problematic, is the characterization of law. Law, in these opinion pieces, was depicted as politics in another form—a tool that can be used by a group to 'wage war'. Nor is this a rare characterization. In recent political debates, particularly in the US, environmental regulation is depicted as a freedom-restricting ideology. There is little focus on the finite capacity of the environment, on the complex reality of environmental problems, or on the detailed and nuanced substance of the law.

As this chapter shows, environmental law is neither a set of magic wands nor a form of crude political power-plays. It is a complex field of legal practice embedded in a legal order that responds to the complexity of environmental problems. The challenges involved in this have been introduced in this chapter, but as we will see there are many more involved in the operation of environmental law.

Chapter 4
The history of environmental law

Environmental law does not emerge overnight. Societies are committed to environmental quality, but in most jurisdictions the creation of environmental laws is a hard-fought battle. It occurs only after the persistence of environmental problems, public outcry, political agitation, the recognition of such problems, and a window of political opportunity. It requires confronting the problems of scientific uncertainty and clashes of values. It also never happens in a vacuum. Environmental problems emerge alongside other political issues—economic growth, crime, foreign affairs—and must be reconciled with old political battle lines. Environmental law has emerged simultaneously at the local, regional, national, and international level.

Industrialization

It is not the case that environmental law is entirely new. Environmental problems have been inherent in civilization since the beginning and have needed collective management. In the 1st century AD there were laws in ancient Imperial China regulating the hunting of birds and the burning of forests. Ancient Rome had laws concerning rubbish and noxious industries such as tanneries. Alongside the Magna Carta in 1217 was the Forest Charter, which governed management of the King's Forests. It was administered through specialized forest courts.

In the 19th century, industrialization and greater population density in growing cities brought with it a whole series of tragedies of the commons. The most obvious were to do with hygiene and human sewage. The UK experience is typical in this regard. In cities of that time, toilets were often open pits. Sewage was left in ditches, large piles, and flowed untreated into rivers from which people obtained their drinking water. The spread of disease was inevitable—31,000 died of cholera in an 1832 outbreak alone. Piecemeal legislation was one response, but wholesale legal reform did not happen until the late 1850s.

The barriers to legislative action were many. There were the limits of knowledge. The spread of cholera is caused by human faeces in water, but at the time this was not understood and the belief was that it was spread through miasmas in the air. In 1853 the *Lancet* stated: 'What is cholera? Is it a fungus, a miasma, an electrical disturbance, a deficiency of ozone, a morbid off-scouring of the intestinal canal? We know nothing. We are at sea in a whirlpool of conjecture.'

The vivid power of John Snow's epidemiological studies in the mid-19th century was important in changing scientific views. In 1855, he mapped the location of deaths from cholera (Figure 3) and thus showed a link between the disease and sources of drinking water.

He was not the only one making this connection, but opinion did not change overnight. While the filth of city streets (and the human faeces in it) was there for all to see, the human health consequences of that filth were less visible. Visibility was ultimately provided by official reports that collected statistics and made the problems clear. The most famous was Edwin Chadwick's *Report on the Sanitary Condition of the Labouring Populations of Great Britain* (1842), which recorded the average life expectancy of a working-class man in Liverpool as fifteen (for a man of the professional classes it was thirty-five).

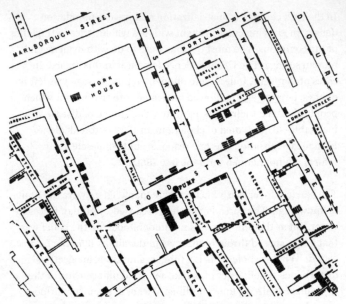

3. John Snow, 'On the Mode of Communication of Cholera' (1855). The black bars show the number of deaths from cholera in Soho, London.

Highlighting these issues did not necessarily make it a political imperative to do something about them. This was particularly true when action would cost ratepayers money, and building new sewers was perceived as giving central government more power, in an era in which they had little. This was unattractive to those who believed in local government and/or no government at all. Ideas of 'public health' were also still embryonic and poor health was often understood as caused by poor morals. Pollution was not just a physical thing, but a cultural one as well.

The passing of Chadwick's Public Health Act in 1848 was a first important step in legislative intervention, but within a decade that initiative had failed. Based on a centralized Benthamite utilitarian logic, it was perceived by many as an anathema to established ideas of decentralized English government. More significant legislative reform occurred in 1858 with London's 'Great Stink'. The putrid smell coming from the Thames was so great that it was described by the *Observer* as 'stinking out the Commons Committee'. By this time, the significance of gathering information and thus the role of central government had been established. Commenting on public health, John Stuart Mill noted in 1859 that central government had a 'distinct role' in a 'liberal society' due to its 'superior intelligence gathering and information processing capacities'.

Alongside the consequences of poor hygiene were the problems caused by industrial activity polluting air, water, and soil, as well as generating hazardous waste. In *Hard Times*, Charles Dickens described a northern industrial town as: 'a town of machinery and tall chimneys, out of which interminable serpents of smoke trailed themselves for ever and ever, and never got uncoiled. It had a black canal in it, and a river that ran purple with ill smelling dye.'

The Reverend Charles Kingsley, who wrote the children's book *The Water Babies*, described pollution in terms of a classic tragedy of the commons in one of his sermons. 'We know well how,' he said, 'in some manufactures, a certain amount of waste is profitable—that it pays better to let substances run to refuse, than to use every product of manufacture—as in a steam mill every atom of soot is so much wasted fuel; but it pays better not to consume the whole fuel and to let the soot escape.'

Kingsley then went on to argue that the same undesirable logic was operating in relation to people. 'Capital is accumulated more rapidly by wasting a certain amount of human life, human health, human intellect.' Pollution thus went hand in hand with a particular strain of Victorian capitalism that not only had implications for the environment, but also for society.

Mid-Victorian parliaments did pass legislation dealing with industrial pollution, but it was not a grand success. Some of it was piecemeal. Alkali works were regulated but there were no general standards for air quality. The success of much of the legislation depended on it being properly enforced by government authorities, but given the small size of government, resources for enforcement did not exist. The problems of England were also evidenced in other industrialized nations.

Nature and well-being

The other front on which environmental law developed was to do with natural landscape. In both England and the US in the second half of the 19th century, a nature conservation movement developed. The focus of this movement was not so much on human health but on the relationship between the natural environment and well-being. It was led by a group of writers who, as Bill McKibben notes, 'invented the grammar and vocabulary of wildness that birthed the environmental movement'.

In the US, Henry David Thoreau's *Walden* (1854) was an ode to nature and a modest and self-sufficient way of life. 'It is a vulgar error to suppose that you have tasted huckleberries who never plucked them.' John Muir followed at the end of the 19th century, his work leading to both the creation of the first comprehensive national parks system in the US and the founding of the non-governmental organization, the Sierra Club. Later Aldo Leopold's writings buttressed the growing conservation movement. While each of these writers took a different approach, they were all encouraging people to reflect on how they understood the world and ways to live in it. In doing so they were questioning the wisdom of the mainstream. 'Education, I fear, is learning to see one thing by going blind to another', wrote Leopold.

The US was not alone. In 1879 the colony of New South Wales created the first Australian National Park (now the Royal National

Park), south of Sydney. In both the US and Australia the contrast between industrialized cities and wilderness was stark. The conservation movement focused on preserving the latter and alternative ways of living. In the UK, there was a thriving movement dedicated to ideals of beauty, as promoted by writers such as John Ruskin. The protection of cultural heritage and animals was also emphasized. These movements had an urban dimension. In the 19th century, writers such as Ebenezer Howard promoted the concept of garden cities—suburban utopias that promised the working classes a better way of life.

Throughout the first half of the 20th century there were further political and legal developments in regards to environmental quality in cities and the natural environment. In part these were shaped by utopian political and artistic movements. Modernism influenced town planning and architecture the world over with its dreams of universal master narratives. The grand boulevards of Paris and the building of the 'Western' cities of the Global South reflected that thinking. But the 20th century was also an era of war and further industrialization. The rebuilding of cities after World War II meant that most European countries needed to develop new town planning regimes that reconciled urgent housing needs with quality of life. Likewise, serious environmental problems such as the Great Fogs of London in the 1950s resulted in legislative responses such as the UK Clean Air Act in 1956.

International developments

The international dimension of environmental problems also became obvious. Environmental problems did not stay within borders, and they also affected commons beyond the jurisdictions of nation states such as the high seas. From the early 1940s onwards, international agreements were signed in relation to whaling (1946), oil pollution (1954), and fishing (1958). Transboundary air pollution between European countries, and between Canada and the US, also became an issue. For example, the emissions of sulphur dioxide and nitrogen oxide in one country were leading to acidification of rainfall in another, and thus to the destruction of forests.

Public international law and international political discourses were still in their infancy however, and dominated by ideas of national sovereignty, particularly when it came to natural resources. As Vaughan Lowe wrote when he was Chichele Professor of Public International Law at Oxford: 'Archetypal international law is concerned with the rights and duties of States towards one another.' In the 19th century, as the international law scholar Dan Bodansky has eloquently put it, that meant it was a subject about 'coexistence rather than co-operation'. Fundamental to that coexistence was the idea of national sovereignty. States consented to be bound by international law, but they were deemed independent of other states, and they were understood to be in control of their own territory.

As environmental problems did not stay within jurisdictional boundaries, further cooperation was required at the international level. The oil crisis in the early 1970s and concerns regarding overpopulation also shaped international policy discourses. Indeed, Hardin's article on the tragedy of the commons was an essay primarily about overpopulation. The main thrust of the article, as described in its one-line abstract, was 'The population problem has no technical solution; it requires a fundamental extension in morality.' The Club of Rome, a global think tank founded in 1968, published *The Limits to Growth* in 1972, a report that examined how economic growth was put at risk if environmental protection was not taken seriously.

The non-binding but symbolically significant Stockholm Declaration on the Human Environment was signed in 1972. Agreements also clustered around specific issues—persistent organic pollutants, migratory birds, world heritage. A still-emerging European Economic Community (EEC) was an example of a more legally robust model of supranational cooperation. The EEC had been created as a 'common market' in 1958 that operated on the basis of free movement of goods, services, and workers, and freedom of establishment. In 1972 at the Paris Summit between heads of the member states it was declared that: 'Economic expansion is not an end in itself.... As befits the genius of Europe, particular attention will be given to intangible values and to protecting the environment so that progress may really be put at the service of mankind.'

A year later the EEC issued its first action programme, and started to pass the first environmental protection directives which by the 1990s numbered in the hundreds. 'A high level of [environmental] protection' thus became a fundamental aim of the EEC and its later incarnations, the European Community and the EU.

New social movements: the 1960s and beyond

During the 1960s a range of new social movements emerged in Western democracies, all of which challenged the authority of governing institutions. Environmentalism emerged alongside the civil rights movement, feminism, gay rights, and political action aimed at ensuring democracies were more democratic. There were multiple strands to this emerging environmental movement. Protection of the environment was mainstream. *Limits to Growth* was understood as a pragmatic call to arms. But environmental issues also sparked a more radical politics. E. F. Schumacher's 1973 collection of essays, *Small Is Beautiful: A Study of Economics As If People Mattered*, argued for a rethink of how society operated. Likewise, new political coalitions were in evidence. In the 1970s, Australian trade unions banned their workers from working on building sites that were viewed as environmentally destructive.

Legal and political agitation was also occurring on multiple fronts. Rachel Carson's *Silent Spring* (1962), a book examining the environmental and human health impacts of pesticide use, became a major catalyst for legislative reform in the US. The Green Revolution had promoted the use of fertilizers and other agricultural technology in the developing world, but critics argued it had led to environmental destruction. The quality of urban spaces also became an issue on the political agenda, often due to a highly centralist approach to town planning promoted by modernism that gave precedence to roads and large-scale development. Jane Jacobs' classic, *The Death and Life of Great American Cities* (1961), was a passionate cry for a different vision of city living; one that was bottom up and focused on vibrant street life.

All this, despite its many disparate sources, resulted in agreement about the importance of environmental protection and thus genuine political momentum. This was the era of comprehensive environmental law reform in many countries, and during this time the foundations of the contemporary structures of environmental law were laid. In most Western countries, environmental governmental ministries were created and environmental legislation passed. In the US for example, in the late 1960s and early 1970s a bipartisan Congress pushed through a series of environmental protection statutes. Environmental law emerged as a subject to be practised and to be taught in law schools.

Sustainable development

Throughout the 1970s, regional and international agreements were signed in relation to a range of pollution and nature conservation issues. There were important successes. By the mid-1980s it had become apparent that the ozone layer was being depleted by a range of different halogenated hydrocarbons. The Vienna Convention (1985) created a framework for international action, and the Montreal Protocol (1987) and subsequent amendments resulted in the phasing out of ozone-depleting substances.

Discourses at the international level were transformed, particularly due to the World Commission on Environment and Development's 1987 report, *Our Common Future*. Known as the Brundtland Report, it put forward the idea of sustainable development—development that 'meets the needs of the present without compromising the needs of future generations to meet their own needs'. While it was quickly appreciated that sustainable development could mean many different things, it was another focal point for bringing diverse groups together in the belief that environmental protection and economic growth were compatible aims that could be harmonized. This was the era of win–win environmental strategies and 'thinking globally, acting locally'.

The Brundtland Report led to the UN Conference on Environment and Development in Rio in 1992. At that event, 172 countries (with 108 heads of state participating) signed up to the Rio Declaration on Environment and Development (Rio Declaration), the UNFCCC, and the UN Convention on Biological Diversity. Alongside these were the Statement of Forest Principles and the comprehensive Agenda 21 programme, which aimed to implement sustainable development at the local level. This was an era of global environmental consensus, in which states cooperated to develop new frameworks to ensure future environmental quality alongside a commitment to development.

One aspect of this was the focus on environmental principles. The Rio Declaration outlined a number of these—intergenerational equity, the polluter pays principle, and the precautionary principle to name a few. It also did other things. Article 11 of the Rio Declaration says that 'States shall enact effective environmental legislation'. The Declaration emphasized access to justice and public participation and resulted in the UN Economic Commission for Europe's Aarhus Convention on Access to Information, Public Participation in Decision-Making and Access to Justice in Environmental Matters (Aarhus Convention).

While not binding (Chapter 5), the Rio Declaration did serve as a source of legal inspiration in a number of jurisdictions. From the 1990s, the Indian Supreme Court made environmental principles a substantive feature of their environmental law jurisprudence, interrelating them with the right to life under the Indian constitution. The Australian government introduced an ambitious strategy on ecologically sustainable development and amended environmental legislation to include environmental principles. The EU, inspired by ideas of sustainable development, introduced new regulatory techniques aimed at harnessing markets in the interests of environmental protection. The EU greenhouse emission trading scheme, first introduced in 2003, was a prime example of this. New Zealand passed the Resource Management Act in 1991—legislation that comprehensively reformed environmental law to make it more coherent.

Disenchantment

None of this was to last. By the 2000s the political alignments that had brought these environmental laws into being began to fall apart. A political reframing occurred and environmental laws began to be seen as a threat to economic growth. In the US, and in a number of other Western jurisdictions, there was a rolling back of environmental laws.

In part this reflected a new deregulatory politics, often derived from neo-liberal thinking. This was most obvious in the US, where environmental regulations were subject to ongoing political and legal attack from those being regulated. One aspect of this was to challenge the scientific basis of environmental actions in an analytically opportunistic way. Given the limits of science in understanding environmental problems this was a particularly effective strategy. Generalists found it hard to distinguish between what was a serious flaw in the scientific analysis underpinning an environmental regulation and what was not. There were also strategies by specific industries of 'manufacturing' further scientific uncertainties as a means of preventing regulation.

But the deregulatory push was not only neo-liberal in nature. The sociologist Arlie Russell Hochschild spent five years interviewing Tea Party supporters in one of the most polluted parts of the US (south-west Louisiana) about why they did not support environmental regulation. Their reasons were varied. One woman was loyal to industry. Another held a belief that you can't have everything and other things were more important. One man saw regulation as akin to 'cement' and that 'the government is almost living our lives for us'. Another had a belief in the free market. For him, 'the EPA stood up for the biological environment, but it was allowing—and it seemed at times it was causing—a cultural erosion'. All of them saw the 'environment' as cutting ahead in the line of those working towards the Great American Dream.

Among other groups, particularly in the Global South, the rise of neo-liberal thinking resulted in growing scepticism about the promises of thinking globally. Rather than being the route to a better world, globalization and in particular the driving logic of the global economy were seen as causes of environmental degradation. Thus, Anna Lowenhaupt Tsing, in a study of Indonesian deforestation, notes that 'Indonesian forests were not destroyed for local needs; their products were taken for the world'. The resulting politics spoke to 'central dilemmas of our times: Why is global capitalism so messy? Who speaks for nature? What kinds of social justice make sense in the twenty-first century?' A similar pattern could be seen in other countries. Environmental justice movements sprung up in developing countries across the world. Arundhati Roy, speaking in 2004, argued for a globalization of dissent that confronted neo-liberal capitalism and its neo-colonial tendencies.

Environmental issues thus became different political symbols in different places. Environmental problems were also now bound up in the supply chains of globalization, but those supply chains often made such problems invisible. The relationship between the manufacturing boom in China, its growing pollution problems, and the flooding of Western economies with a variety of goods, was not as obvious as it should have been.

Climate change and the Anthropocene

Alongside this disenchantment emerged a more serious environmental problem—climate change. This is the ultimate tragedy of the commons. It is a global, collective issue that scholar Mike Hulme describes as a 'wicked problem' that defies 'rational and optimal solutions', as it is 'beyond the reach of mere technical knowledge and traditional forms of governance'. The scholar Steve Rayner notes that '[c]limate change is not so much a discrete problem to be solved as it is a condition under which human beings will have to make choices about such matters as priorities for economic development and the way we govern ourselves'. The politics of climate change are in many ways the politics of earlier environmental problems, transposed to the global stage.

It is not an issue ignored by states. At the international level, the UNFCCC and its subsequent agreements have created a framework for international cooperation and action. Many countries have also introduced legislation to mitigate climate change and to adapt to it. Likewise, there are countless examples of regional and local initiatives. Given the widespread causes and effects of climate change these legal reforms relate to a range of topics, including energy, transport, building standards, town planning, and agriculture. As the conference discussed in Chapter 3 highlighted, there have been many court cases as well.

For many scholars and commentators, climate change is evidence of the fact that we have entered the age of the Anthropocene. This geological term, coined by the scientists Paul Crutzen and Eugene

Stoermer, connotes the way in which humans have become the most significant ecological force on the planet due to energy use and population growth. We are in an era of new uncertainties and new risks. This new era is understood as a product of capitalism and its accompanying intellectual frames. J. R. McNeill and Peter Engelke, commenting on the Anthropocene, criticize 'academic social scientists and humanists' for their retreat from 'grimy and greasy realities into various never-never lands', while economists have 'jilted reality' for 'ever-more-abstract modelling based on universalising assumptions of individual behaviour and state conduct, casually ripped from all historical and cultural, not to mention ecological context'.

The expansion of political imagination

These harsh words are a reminder that environmental problems are very real, and in recent years it has been scientists who have identified the seriousness of environmental problems. It is also a reminder that intellectual disciplines and political thought have an important role in framing the world. There is another dimension to those harsh words. As Rebecca Solnit states: 'physics is inevitable; if you put more carbon dioxide into the atmosphere, the planet warms and as the planet warms, various kinds of chaos and ruin are loosed. Politics, on the other hand, is not inevitable.' Indeed, the history of environmental law has been a history of expanding the political imagination. While politics is not inevitable, it is shaped by what is imagined to be politically possible. What was imagined possible in 1848 is not the same as in 2017.

The political theorist Yaron Ezrahi has described political imagining as: 'that of composing, decomposing, and recomposing the fabrics of images, metaphors, narratives, symbols, metaphysics, fantasies, commonsense facts, popular views of science, social values, shared fears and emotions, and other cultural and experiential materials'. All of this can be seen in the history

49

of environmental law. Political imagining is not only about environmental problems and how to address them. It is also about how we imagine the social world and the physical world and the relationships between them. Specifically it is about what we understand as acceptable and unacceptable ways for a community to live. This is the stuff of politics, and it is also the stuff of law.

Chapter 5
Expanding legal imagination

Just as political imagination has had to expand to address
environmental problems, so too has legal imagination.
Chapter 3 showed that environmental law involves the deliberate
development of legal systems to respond to the complexity of
environmental problems while ensuring the stability of legal
systems. The creation and operation of environmental law has
forced lawyers to reflect upon, and develop, legal concepts, rules,
and principles. This is because environmental law is not confined
to the world of contract law in which two parties are legally bound
by an agreement—an agreement which manages their legal
expectations, obligations, and rights. Legal imagination is needed
to develop law to respond to a world of multiple interconnected
parties, scientific uncertainty, and socio-political conflict.

International environmental law

There are many examples of the ways in which environmental
problems and environmental law force imaginative reflection on
the part of environmental lawyers. The growth of international
agreements is one such example. Public international law
originated as a body of *general* law between nation states. In
contrast, the signing of specific agreements in response to
particular environmental problems led to what international law
scholars describe as 'fragmentation'. Environmental problems

were not the only cause of fragmentation, but like trade law and human rights law, piecemeal legal responses result in international law becoming a field of differentiated areas of law making and institutional practice. In the opinion of the International Law Commission, fragmentation results in 'conflicts between rules or rule systems, deviating institutional practices, and possibly, the loss of an overall perspective on law'.

Fragmentation manifests itself in a range of ways. For example, in the 2000s a legal dispute between Ireland and the UK over radioactive emissions from an English nuclear reprocessing plant could have been adjudicated upon by three different tribunals under three different regimes: the UN Convention of the Law of the Sea; the Convention for the Protection of the Marine Environment of the North-East Atlantic; and the various treaties of the EU. As the international law scholar Martti Koskenniemi notes, each regime governs the same set of facts and thus there is no obvious answer to the question of which should be determinative.

Many international environmental agreements require some form of regime to accompany them, whether through the creation of a committee or some form of networked administrative structure. These regimes often have multi-level aspects—as with the Rio Declaration they encourage national reform. Like fragmentation, these reforms have also transformed the international law landscape.

The UNFCCC 1992 is a good example of this. The convention is very much a framework convention, which recognizes a problem, sets goals, but most importantly empowers further action, specifically through meetings of the Conference of Parties (COP). The Kyoto Protocol (1997), the Marrakesh Accords (2001), the Cancun Agreements (2010), and the Paris Agreement (2015) are all outcomes of COP processes. The Clean Development Mechanism created as part of the Kyoto Protocol allows industrialized countries to receive legal credit for investing in clean development projects in developing countries. Such a scheme needs to be administered however. Alongside the UNFCCC is the separate structure of the IPCC, which was founded in 1988 by the World Meteorological Organization and the United Nations Environment Programme (UNEP). It provides an overview of scientific understandings of climate change.

There are many other examples. Article 15 of the Aarhus Convention requires the creation of 'optional arrangements of a non-confrontational, non-judicial and consultative nature for reviewing compliance with the provisions of the Convention', and this led to the creation of a compliance committee. The 1972 World Heritage Convention is administered by a committee that decides what is on the World Heritage List. Within the UN, the UNEP has also been developed. Moreover, traditional international bodies such as the UN General Assembly, the Organisation for Economic Co-operation and Development, and the World Bank have expanded their remit to cover environmental issues.

There has also been the development of novel legal obligations and regimes in the international environmental law sphere. Many environmental agreements contain non-binding obligations, what international lawyers call 'soft law'. This is because while states are willing to cooperate, they are keen to protect their sovereignty. Take the international environmental law scholar Lavanya Rajamani's description of the 2015 Paris Agreement, the latest evolutionary step in the UNFCCC process. It is 'a curious instrument', she writes:

> Albeit a treaty within the meaning of the Vienna Convention on the Law of Treaties, the Paris Agreement is littered with provisions that either have weak normative content or seem to be wholly lacking in it. These provisions do not create rights and obligations for States, as one would expect operational provisions of a treaty to do, rather they provide context, offer reassurances and construct narratives.

Given the fact that climate change is a global problem that requires action at all levels of government and a change of thinking, this legal framework makes sense, particularly in light of the evolution of the UNFCCC regime since 1992. The Paris Agreement is 'curious' not from that perspective, but from a public international law one. Despite its curious nature, it is also still international law, and in being so requires international lawyers to reflect on the nature and scope of the subject. Not surprisingly leading scholars often talk of the need to reimagine the subject in light of these developments.

Nuisance law

That process of reimagination is also seen in national legal systems in regards to both legislation and case law. The development of tort law is a good example of the latter. Tort law is the law of civil wrongs and includes laws such as the law of trespass, negligence, and public and private nuisance. Let me focus on the last of these in the English context.

Private nuisance is a common law tort doctrine that has existed since at least the 13th century. It requires that one landowner will not unreasonably interfere with another's use or enjoyment of their land. Only those with interests in property can bring nuisance actions. In bringing such an action they need to show that interference is an 'unreasonable interference'. They need to show that the person they are bringing the action against is responsible for the interference. A nuisance action usually ends in a particular remedy—an injunction—a court order stopping the nuisance. The careful application of these different elements of nuisance by a common law court ensures its stability and coherence. It makes the law, in Waldron's terms, 'calculable' (Chapter 3). Indeed, many scholars see these different tests as inherent in the structure of private nuisance due to it being a tort protecting interests in property.

Pollution is something that obviously could amount to a private nuisance. A factory emitting smoke would seem to be an unreasonable interference with the use and enjoyment of a neighbour's land. But applying the doctrine to pollution cases raises a number of questions, the most obvious being what amounts to an 'unreasonable interference'. As the case law makes clear that depends on the nature of the locality. That is a question of fact, but one shaped by a whole series of legal doctrines. What is unreasonable in an area with many factories is very different from a wholly rural area. Just because there is pollution does not mean that the interference is unreasonable.

In the modern era, difficult questions also arise about the interaction between private nuisance and planning law and/or regulatory authorization for a particular activity. If a waste disposal tip has a pollution permit to operate can it be an 'unreasonable interference'? The current answer in English law is that it can be. But planning law can affect the nature of a locality in some circumstances, and in other circumstances statutory regimes have prevented actions in nuisance being brought.

In these different cases, the legal nature of private nuisance and the wordings and purposes of these different statutory schemes are important. Lawyers' arguments are structured around both, as is the reasoning in many pages in many judgments. That is not surprising—it preserves the internal coherence of nuisance as a legal doctrine and thus its stability and calculability. This is not to say the tort of private nuisance does not develop as a doctrine. Law cannot be static. Every legal action brought arguably raises questions about a doctrine's stability and coherence. But the process of legal evolution is a careful and thoughtful one.

Even if a private nuisance action is successful it has its limitations. Private nuisance also can only be brought against identifiable defendants. It is thus not particularly effective at addressing large-scale pollution problems with multiple polluters. Likewise, usually nuisance actions can only be brought after the interference has occurred.

Private nuisance actions have thus never been a significant feature of environmental law. Other legal frameworks needed to be developed. During the 19th century, public health legislation in the UK used the structure of nuisance as a basis for passing legislation that created a new form of nuisance—statutory nuisance. The law of statutory nuisance still exists today and gives local authorities powers to deal with local environmental problems. What amounts to a statutory nuisance is defined by a list set out in a statute. In England and Wales it includes 'any premises in such a state as to be prejudicial to health or a nuisance' and 'any dust, steam, smell or other effluvia arising on industrial, trade or business premises and being prejudicial to health or a nuisance'. While a powerful tool in small-scale cases, statutory nuisance has the same structural limitations that private nuisance has.

Criminal law

A similar pattern of needing to reflect on existing law can be seen in relation to criminal law. A common feature of pollution legislation in many jurisdictions is that it creates criminal offences for polluting. Any such offence needs to be interpreted and applied to specific circumstances. In doing so the question arises regarding what legal principles apply.

Take a simple water pollution offence from British legislation in the 1990s: 'A person contravenes this section if he causes or knowingly permits any poisonous, noxious or polluting matter or any solid waste matter to enter any controlled waters.' What does it mean to 'cause or knowingly permit'? In 1998 the UK House of Lords concluded in *Empress Car Company (Abertillery) Ltd v National Rivers Authority* that:

the prosecution need not prove that the defendant did something which was the *immediate* cause of the pollution: maintaining tanks, lagoons or sewage systems full of noxious liquid is doing something, even if the immediate cause of the pollution was lack of maintenance, a natural event or the act of a third party.

That last phrase was important in this case because a factory was claiming that they had not 'caused' poisonous, noxious, or polluting matter to enter water, but that an unknown third person had done so by turning on a tap.

The House of Lords' test makes sense from an environmental protection perspective. The broad definition of 'cause' means that factories cannot escape criminal liability by blaming someone else. A third party may be the direct cause of the pollution, but the failure of the factory to stop them was also a 'cause' and thus the factory is also guilty of an offence. This then encourages factories to operate on the basis that vandals might break in, and thus take precautionary measures such as creating environmental management systems to stop that occurring.

The case is problematic for some criminal lawyers however. For this group, to find someone guilty of a criminal offence it is important that ideas of fault be inherent in tests of causation. Fault is not relevant to the test in *Empress Car*. A leading English criminal law textbook describes the reasoning in the case as 'both contrary to principle and law', particularly because the case, in making the factory liable for someone else's act, is undermining the importance that English criminal law places on attributing criminal responsibility only in cases where a person has acted autonomously. For these authors the ruling in *Empress Car* 'disempowers' defendants. Other commentators and judges have understood the case as being about environmental regulation and thus not the basis for any more widely applicable principle. The logic of dealing with environmental problems is understood as distinct from established ideas of criminal responsibility. There is no simple way of determining whether these different approaches are right or wrong. A simple criminal offence thus gives rise to a tricky set of legal questions.

Environmental impact assessment

Sometimes the law created to address environmental problems is completely novel. Take environmental impact assessment (EIA). The National Environmental Policy Act 1969 (NEPA) in the US was the first statute to introduce it, and since then variations on EIA can be seen in nearly all regimes throughout the world. In 2010 the International Court of Justice even recognized a duty in international law to undertake an EIA in cases of transboundary harm.

Each EIA regime is a legislated regime with a specific set of obligations. NEPA requires that for 'every recommendation or report on proposals for legislation and other major Federal actions significantly affecting the quality of the human environment, a detailed statement by the responsible official' must be provided on:

(i) the environmental impact of the proposed action,

(ii) any adverse environmental effects which cannot be avoided should the proposal be implemented,

(iii) alternatives to the proposed action,

(iv) the relationship between local short-term uses of man's environment and the maintenance and enhancement of long-term productivity, and

(v) any irreversible and irretrievable commitments of resources which would be involved in the proposed action should it be implemented.

This is a dry read, but even on the most cursory review what is clear is that it is a very different type of law from a private nuisance action or a pollution offence. One of the aims of NEPA is 'to create and maintain conditions under which man and nature can exist in productive harmony'. The US environmental law scholar, William Rodgers, has described it as the Magna Carta of US environmental law. But what type of law is it?

The main thrust of the legislation is that it places a legal obligation on a government agency to assess the environmental impact of proposed legislation or 'major federal actions' that 'significantly affect' the environment. This is a proactive way of dealing with environmental problems before they become problems. As a legal obligation, it is a legal world away from the contractual obligations between Herman and Frank (Chapter 3). There are no rights owed to another party, but rather a duty to act in a specific way and carry out a particular form of analysis. As Yale law professor, Jerry Mashaw, described it, it is a law from an 'activist state—a state that emphasizes the administration of social and economic life in pursuit of collective ends'. Such a state, he claims, 'tend[s] to redefine rights in ways that de-emphasize individual legal remedies'. And that is something that raises many legal questions about what this type of legal obligation means. As a US judge described it, NEPA 'set the law ablaze'.

It did so in many different ways. For a lawyer the most obvious question was whether this created any judicially enforceable duty. The rapid answer of the US courts was that it did. The procedural provisions 'created a strict standard of compliance'. That then gave rise to questions about the nature of those procedural provisions, and when they would apply. Courts were thus required to interpret what a 'major Federal action' was and what 'significantly affecting the quality of the human environment' meant. NEPA also vested in the Council on Environmental Quality, a central government agency, a coordinating power and the power to develop guidelines. Questions are thus raised about the legal status and significance of these. There are also issues to do with how the duties under NEPA interrelate with other pieces of legislation. It is thus not surprising that NEPA gave rise to a rich body of case law, as has similar legislation in other jurisdictions.

Most of that case law concerns screening—how a decision-maker should determine whether a project is likely to have a significant effect on the environment and thus require an EIA. This classificatory issue is difficult as it raises mixed questions of legal interpretation and factual application. Moreover, the test applies to future impacts. The reason for the large amount of litigation in relation to screening is that the classificatory process at the screening stage is pivotal and has practical implications. If it is decided that an EIA is required, then environmental impacts must be studied in detail and consulted upon. This process is often the only way in which third parties can influence a particular activity. On the other hand, the decision to do an EIA will usually impose extra costs on the proponent of an activity and slow down the decision-making process. There is also no doubt that the decision that action requires an EIA has a symbolic aspect—it is a signal that the state has decided that this particular activity requires extra scrutiny. The political struggles of environmental law thus transform into a set of complex legal questions.

Standing and access to courts

Let me give one final example of these struggles with legal imagination. In 1972 the US law professor, Christopher Stone, wrote an article with a title that always makes my students giggle: 'Should Trees Have Standing?' The giggling reflects the way in which environmental problems raise 'curious' legal questions. But to explain that you need some backstory.

In most legal systems, people can challenge the actions of a government administration in a court to ensure such actions are within the power of that administrative body. The action is described as a judicial review action and it plays a big role in environmental law (see Chapter 7). Historically, to bring a judicial review action in most legal systems you needed to show that your individual rights had been affected by the administrative action. This is called the doctrine of standing. Asylum applicants who have been turned down, developers who have had their planning applications refused, and veterans who have been denied social security benefits will have standing. General members of the public will not however. The reasons given for this standing requirement are many: to prevent frivolous actions; to stop the court being flooded with cases; to ensure that courts do not become political forums; and that the requirement of such a right is inherent in judicial review.

Whatever the case, challenging administrative action because of its environmental impact raises a conundrum in relation to standing. Environmental impacts are usually widespread and affect everyone. They can also occur in wilderness where no individual is affected. Applying the standard standing doctrine to environmental cases often results in a situation where no one can bring an action.

This was the dilemma that faced the US Supreme Court in the 1972 case *Sierra Club v Morton*. The Sierra Club had been founded by John Muir in the 19th century, and was made up of members interested in the conservation of protected areas of the US. The case involved the Sierra Club challenging the federal government for authorizing the Disney Corporation to build a $35 million ski resort in a remote part of the Sierra Nevada Mountains called Mineral King Valley (Figure 4). The valley was part of a game refuge, and the Sierra Club's legal argument was that the federal government had failed to comply with its own laws. To bring that action, however, they needed to establish standing. The lower court had found they had none because they had 'to show more of a direct interest'. The Supreme Court reconsidered this question.

In this case, standing was regulated by a legislative provision which stated: 'A person suffering legal wrong because of agency action, or adversely affected or aggrieved by agency action within the meaning of a relevant statute, is entitled to judicial review thereof.'

4. Mineral King Valley, California.

In previous cases the Supreme Court recognized that 'palpable economic injuries' could be the basis for standing, and also allowed standing when 'the challenged action had caused [a party] "injury in fact"' and where the alleged injury was to an interest 'arguably within the zone of interests to be protected or regulated' by the statutes that the agencies were claimed to have violated. These were all broad tests, but did not cover the Sierra Club, who were arguing that the development would destroy the scenery of the park and enjoyment of it for future generations.

The majority of judges in the Supreme Court concluded that the Sierra Club did not have standing. They stated:

> Aesthetic and environmental well-being, like economic well-being, are important ingredients of the quality of life in our society, and the fact that particular environmental interests are shared by the many rather than the few does not make them less deserving of legal protection through the judicial process. But the 'injury in fact' test requires more than an injury to a cognizable interest. It requires that the party seeking review be himself among the injured.

Granting standing to those that did not have a 'direct stake' in the outcome would have allowed actions where groups did 'no more than vindicate their own value preferences through the judicial process'.

In dissent, Justice Blackmun highlighted that this was no 'ordinary, run-of-the-mill litigation' and it raised the question about the importance of protecting the environment. He asked: 'Must our law be so rigid and our procedural concepts so inflexible that we render ourselves helpless when the existing methods and the traditional concepts do not quite fit and do not prove to be entirely adequate for new issues?' This was particularly when the issues the Sierra Club were raising were not 'shallow or perfunctory' from a legal perspective. For Justice Blackmun, standing could either be established by the Sierra Club amending their legal documents so they complied with the majority's standing requirements (which he thought they could), or by 'an imaginative expansion' of the traditional concept of standing so as to encompass this case.

The other dissenting judge, Justice Douglas, took another approach:

> The critical question of 'standing' would be simplified and also put neatly in focus if we fashioned a federal rule that allowed environmental issues to be litigated before federal agencies or federal courts in the name of the inanimate object about to be despoiled, defaced, or invaded by roads and bulldozers and where injury is the subject of public outrage.

Put simply, objects in the natural environment should be able to bring legal actions in their own names. His argument was explicitly influenced by Stone's article that was a legal brief in the case.

This is when the giggling always starts, as students begin to imagine some Monty Pythonesque comedy sketch with trees standing stalwartly in court making their legal arguments. But as Justice

Douglas pointed out, inanimate objects—corporations and ships in particular—are often parties to litigation and no one raises an eyebrow. Stone revealed many years later that the inspiration for the argument came from teaching a property law class in which he was musing on the evolution of legal systems. Justice Douglas obviously had the importance of environmental protection in mind—his judgment ends with a quote from Aldo Leopold—but the question he was confronted with was a legal question. The Sierra Club took up Justice Blackmun's suggestion of reframing their legal argument. After further litigation Disney withdrew their application.

In the US, Stone's argument has never held much sway, primarily because the doctrine of standing was expanded in other ways. Likewise, in the US and other countries, environmental legislation often now grants explicit rights to a member of the public to enforce environmental legislation. In 2012, Lord Hope of the UK Supreme Court, in considering the question of standing and arguing a need for a broad test, considered a hypothetical case of the flight of an osprey (Figure 5) to and from 'its favourite fishing

5. Osprey.

loch' being impeded by the building of wind turbines. For him, to limit the standing test to those whose individual property rights were involved would be

> contrary to the purpose of environmental law, which proceeds on the basis that the quality of the natural environment is of legitimate concern to everyone. The osprey has no means of taking that step on its own behalf, any more than any other wild creature. If its interests are to be protected someone has to be allowed to speak up on its behalf.

This factual issue was not relevant to the case before him, but Lord Hope's statement was no longer radical. For many years in the UK, as a matter of practice, groups and individuals have brought legal actions to protect the environment.

Few of my students giggle at allowing someone to speak for ospreys. They shrug their shoulders, as Lord Hope's statements are consistent with the general commitment of the UK Supreme Court to the rule of law and thus to ensuring that government acts within, and not outside, its power. Law has developed, it has adapted to environmental problems, and in doing so legal imaginations have been transformed.

Chapter 6
The significance of nation states

Environmental problems transcend the boundaries of nation states. That fact is a reminder of the physical reality of such problems, and the first pictures of Earth from space are often credited with triggering environmental action because they do not show national boundaries. With that said, the significance of nation states is a songline that forges meaning—a set of legal practices that frame legal understandings of what is possible and what is impossible in relation to environmental law.

This is because, for good or ill, political and legal imagination is the product of political communities that cluster into nation states. Indeed, the late Benedict Anderson described nation states as 'imagined communities' in which the concept of community is 'imagined as a deep, horizontal comradeship'. While jurisdictional lines can be geographically arbitrary, the boundaries of imagined national communities are understood as being more legally robust. True, those boundaries shift, and can shift dramatically, but at any point in time they delineate what territory is within a nation's sovereign power and thus what the governing body of that political community has legal authority over.

Anderson was pointing to the significance of nation states for political thought, but concepts of nation states also dominate legal thought, particularly the legal heritage of the Western world.

As the legal theorist William Twining notes, that tradition 'concentrates on the municipal law of sovereign states, mainly those in advanced industrial societies'. The picture of the world that gives meaning to environmental law is thus not of Earth from space, but the world divided up into jurisdictional entities.

Legal cultures

Nation states thus structure the world. They are the communities around which political and legal responses to environmental problems coalesce. Environmental law is shaped by the legal culture of nation states. A legal culture is made up of the legal system, its norms, its doctrines, its rules and institutions, as well as its animating ideas and aspirations. Legal cultures are 'thick' cultural phenomena that exist separately from political cultures, but also overlap with them. Legal cultures differ between nations and do so in a range of ways.

Countries such as France and Germany have civil law systems, where the emphasis is on comprehensive legislative codes, with courts playing a secondary role. This means that much of the focus of environmental law in these countries is on detailed legislation and the principles and hierarchies such legislation puts in place. In contrast the UK, the Commonwealth, and the US have common law systems in which courts develop legal precedent through adversarial processes. Courts thus play a major role in the development of environmental law alongside environmental legislation. With that said, the courts of civil law systems are usually inquisitorial and thus judges play an interventionist role in adjudicating disputes. This is in contrast to common law systems, which are adversarial and thus rely heavily on parties for the production of evidence and the development of legal arguments.

The internal constitutional arrangements of a country are also fundamental to how environmental law develops in a particular legal culture. The Australian constitution vests all lawmaking power in state governments, unless it is explicitly allocated to the federal government. The general power to protect the environment has not been so allocated. The federal government can act, however, if an environmental problem relates to one of the federal government's explicit legislative powers. The federal government's 'external affairs' power has been an important legal source of power in relation to environmental protection due to the existence of international environmental law.

That power was at the heart of a lengthy High Court of Australia case in 1983 (the *Tasmanian Dams* case), which upheld the federal government's use of the World Heritage Convention to stop the Tasmanian government damming the Franklin River and flooding wilderness. The federal government's Environmental Protection and Biodiversity Conservation Act 1999 has as its object the protection of 'matters of national environmental significance'. The key word here is 'national'—a word with constitutional significance. Due to the federal government's constitutional competences, the matters that fall into that category are issues of environmental significance that relate to specific international agreements, such as the World Heritage Convention or the Ramsar Convention on Wetlands, as they trigger the federal government's 'external affairs' power.

This constitutional framework means that most environmental laws in Australia are enacted by state legislatures. As natural resources are also within state jurisdiction and many states are economically dependent on mineral and energy extraction, the conflict between primary industry and environmental protection has been a tension in Australian environmental law. States seek to both promote resource economies and protect the environment. While there has been a committed process of Australian states and the federal government cooperating in relation to environmental issues, this process is ultimately limited by the constitution.

India is also a federal state, but one in which the constitution vests concurrent powers in state and central governments, unless stated otherwise in the constitution. Despite the concurrent competences, Indian environmental law has developed in a centralized way. Moreover, in contrast to the Australian constitution, the Indian constitution entrenches a series of rights including the right to life in Article 21. That right has been interpreted to include a right to a clean environment. This has resulted in the Indian Supreme Court playing a major role in Indian environmental law.

Within the political community of the UK, there is no written constitution, but the legal relationship between national and local government is a key feature of environmental law architecture. Much environmental legislation is national, but applies, operates, and is enforced at the local level. Planning legislation empowers local planning authorities to determine planning applications in the first instance. Likewise, section 78B(1)(a) of the Environmental Protection Act 1990 states that 'Every local authority shall cause its area to be inspected from time to time for the purpose of identifying contaminated land.'

The asymmetrical devolution of powers to Wales and Scotland since 1998 has also shaped environmental law, as both jurisdictions have developed their own legal regimes in relation to certain issues. With that said, given that many environmental law obligations originally derive from EU law, many of these regimes do similar things. The EU referendum in June 2016 changes that, although at the time of writing it is unclear precisely what effects it will have.

The EU originated with the Treaty of Rome in 1958 between six member states and has grown to have twenty-eight as of the end of 2016. While originating as an international regime, it has evolved over time to be a *sui generis* multi-level governance regime. Article 192 of the Treaty of the Functioning of the European Union (TFEU) gives competence to the EU for environmental protection, but it is shared with member states, who also have a significant role to play in formulating, voting on, and implementing environmental laws. In particular, most environmental law is in the form of directives that member states need to integrate into their legal systems to become law. Directives are also primarily enforced by national courts. Thus, while the same environmental norms are enforced across the EU, the legal operation of those norms is shaped by the legal culture of the individual member states.

In New Zealand, the Resource Management Act 1991 (Chapter 4) explicitly requires any decision-maker exercising power under the act to take into account the principles of the Treaty of Waitangi. The treaty was originally signed between British settlers and the indigenous Maori population in 1840 and legal principles have developed to reflect it. This has meant that Maori thought is an important aspect of New Zealand environmental law. In contrast, in Australia and the US there were no similar legal arrangements, even though both have significant indigenous populations, and thus their environmental law contains no such thinking.

Legal reasoning and legal culture

Beyond these important structural differences between legal cultures there are also more substantive ones. Even in legal cultures that have much in common, there can be differences in legal reasoning and approach. A good example of this is the way in which courts in different jurisdictions have developed (or not developed) environmental principles. As discussed in Chapter 4, environmental principles were included in the Rio Declaration, but they have taken on divergent legal lives in legal cultures.

Australian courts have developed a dense body of case law around environmental principles. While some of this trend can be explained by the inclusion of environmental principles in Australian legislation, it also reflects a strong commitment to legal formalism in Australia—that is, a commitment to resolving disputes through the application of formal legal concepts. Specialist environmental courts (Chapter 9) have played a role in this process as they have the legal skills to incubate and nurture a body of legal doctrine.

In contrast, UK legal reasoning is more pragmatic—there is less emphasis on the articulation of legal doctrine and more upon the adjudication of disputes. As such, environmental principles have not given rise to a rich body of case law. In the 1990s a barrister noted that environmental principles were perhaps too 'rarefied for the English judicial palate'. That is going too far. UK courts do consider environmental principles, but there is less emphasis on articulating their precise legal nature in detail.

The reasoning of the Indian Supreme Court with regard to environmental principles is different again due to its constitutional aspect. It has also been inspired by international law developments. Thus, in *Vellore Citizens Welfare Forum v Union of India* (1996) the court used the international law concept of 'sustainable development' as a launching point for developing environmental principles in Indian environmental law. The court also concluded that the precautionary principle and the polluter pays principle 'are part of the environmental law of the country'. Their logic for doing so was grounded in Article 21 of the Indian Constitution, and in the vast amount of post-independence legislation enacted to protect the environment and the new institutions created to oversee such legislation. Their reasoning thus focused on how the architecture of Indian environmental legislation gives rise to a set of legal concepts. This is very distinct from the Australian approach. The Indian Supreme Court has also developed an ongoing supervisory jurisdiction in many of these cases as a way to address institutional failures.

The Court of Justice of the European Union (CJEU) has also developed a body of case law concerning environmental principles, due to the inclusion of the principles in the EU treaties. One of the most significant tasks of the CJEU is providing authoritative interpretations of EU law. Judgments are required to be translated into all the official languages of the EU, and they are also written by a chamber of judges drawn from the member states. This results in judgments focusing far more on the articulation of the law than the flow of legal argument. As one of my students once put it to me, CJEU judgments 'read as if they are instructions for your new DVD player'—statements of functional imperatives translated in and out of many languages. The interpretative approach of the CJEU is also purposive—the starting point for legal analysis is the aims of a specific environmental law.

In contrast, environmental principles have played virtually no role in legal reasoning in the US. This is primarily due to the fact that international environmental law has had little influence in that jurisdiction. It has also been heavily influenced by legal realism in that there is a focus on the outcome of decisions. This also means that the reasoning in judgments frequently has an explicitly normative flavouring.

Take the US Supreme Court case of *Rapanos v US* (2006), in which the question was how the term 'navigable waters' should be defined in the Clean Water Act. Rapanos had filled in wetlands near a series of ditches that entered into rivers. If what they had filled in was 'navigable waters' they needed a permit from the US Army Corps of Engineers.

Justice Scalia delivered the deciding opinion for the court in which he found the wetlands did not come under that definition. Other judges dissented. The opinions of the different judges turned on what they understood as the legal meaning of the term and the reasoning in previous judgments. At the same time, however, the reasoning of the judges was explicitly influenced by their views of the role of government.

Justice Scalia noted: 'In deciding whether to grant or deny a permit, the US Army Corps of Engineers (Corps) exercises the discretion of an enlightened despot, relying on such factors as "economics," "aesthetics," "recreation," and "in general, the needs and welfare of the people".' He was thus concerned to limit the power of the Corps.

In contrast, Justice Breyer in dissent recognized that the Clean Water Act vested power in the Corps, that the court needed to respect: 'If one thing is clear, it is that Congress intended the Army Corps of Engineers to make the complex technical judgments that lie at the heart of the present cases (subject to deferential judicial review).'

Justice Stevens, also in dissent, thought Justice Scalia's concerns with despotism were needless. He took a purposive approach to legal interpretation. He commented that 'By curtailing the Corps' jurisdiction of more than 30 years, the plurality needlessly jeopardizes the quality of our waters.'

Reading these statements it is easy to think that the judges are 'political' and their judgments are driven solely by their political views on government and environmental protection. This is not the case. What is occurring is that different normative views about legitimate government action are informing legal reasoning.

'Nation-ness' at the international level

Beyond the nation state, the 'cultural artefact' of 'nation-ness', to use Benedict Anderson's terminology, is still in operation. It has shaped the focus of international environmental law, its structures, and its substance. Nation state sovereignty is the fundamental building block of international law. The fluttering flags outside the UN building in New York (Figure 6) are a good example of this.

6. **Flags outside the United Nations Secretariat Building, New York.**

An international agreement is a consenting agreement between the sovereign states that sign it. State sovereignty also confers control to a nation state over its natural resources. But as the legal scholar Phoebe Okowa notes, this requires states to 'respect equally the sovereignty of others and refrain from conduct that may be injurious to other states in a manner that is contrary to the rules of international law'. Historically, international environmental treaties and conventions were thus concerned with environmental problems which required nation states to interact: transboundary issues such as pollution and species protection, and tragedies of the global commons such as climate change and marine pollution.

There are international environmental law agreements moving beyond these functional categories to encompass more general commitments to environmental protection, commitments that often regulate activities internal to a national state. The Rio Declaration is a prime example. But as Bodansky notes in relation to the general commitments of the Stockholm Declaration on

Environment and Development, these are 'part of the larger process by which environmental protection became part of the definition of what it means to be a modern nation state'. Moreover, the ongoing commitment to nation state sovereignty is reflected in the softer form of many of these legal obligations.

As with national legal systems, international law is a distinctive legal culture with its own modes of legal reasoning and its own institutions. International treaties cannot properly be understood without reference to the Vienna Convention on the Law of Treaties, which provides a framework for how treaties are formulated and interpreted. For example, Article 31 states: 'A treaty shall be interpreted in good faith in accordance with the ordinary meaning to be given to the terms of the treaty in their context and in the light of its object and purpose.' This has an important influence on legal reasoning in the international law realm. It is a world away from the legal reasoning of the US Supreme Court.

But it is also the case that the power of courts in the international realm differs in other ways. Thus, while there is a multitude of international courts and tribunals, most relate to specific international agreements. Moreover, none has compulsory jurisdiction in the way that a national court has. Nation states are sovereign powers, a legal fact embedded in the legal culture of international law.

Global trade

In a globalized world, a focus on nation states may appear old fashioned. Globalization is many things, but one of its most significant aspects has been the interconnections between people in different countries through trade. Supply chains for goods cross continents, and in doing so nation states seemingly recede into the background. One-third of the flowers sold in the EU come from Kenya (Chapter 2). Timber from forests logged in Indonesia is shipped to the US.

But nation states never really disappear from this global picture. It is not that global trade is unshackled from nation states. Thus, the Kenyan flower industry is not selling their flowers into a disembodied space—their products will need to comply with the laws and demands of the EU market, just as any product sold in any country will need to comply with the national laws of that country. Markets are created by 'imagined political communities' that enact laws that define how markets operate and what can be sold on them.

Environmental laws are part of this process of market definition. National environmental laws will specify what features a product must have so that it can be sold on a national market. For example, the vehicle emissions laws of any jurisdiction will usually apply to both vehicles manufactured in that jurisdiction and to those imported into it. But in some cases, environmental laws will regulate how a product is produced even if it is produced in another country. Thus, in 2016 the US government published delegated legislation that implemented the Magnuson–Stevens Fishery Conservation and Management Act's prohibition

> on the import and trade, in interstate or foreign commerce, of
> fish taken, possessed, transported or sold in violation of any foreign
> law or regulation or in contravention of a treaty or a binding
> conservation measure of a regional fishery organization to which
> the United States is a party.

The twenty-four pages of the rule thus define what fish can be sold on the US market.

These are examples of where a nation state may impose environmental protection standards. There are many examples of the opposite. In a bid to make their countries more attractive for economic investment, a nation state may lower environmental quality standards as there is a perception that these add to the cost of doing business. If forestry is cheaper to do in Indonesia than in Australia then Indonesia can gain a competitive economic edge on the global market. Problems can then arise when local people are those who predominantly bear the brunt of lower environmental standards. This is the classic problem of a race to the bottom. Nation states compete to attract industry (which brings jobs and tax revenue) by creating advantageous market conditions that allow producers to externalize environmental costs.

Market-making is the activity of nation states, but it does not only occur at the national level. Nation states create markets that transcend nation state borders by signing regional and international trade agreements that liberalize trade. As national environmental laws define what can be sold in a market they can potentially act as barriers to trade.

International trade agreements such as the General Agreement on Tariffs and Trade (GATT) of the World Trade Organization (WTO) do allow signatory members to maintain measures that are 'necessary to protect human, animal or plant life or health' or that relate 'to the conservation of exhaustible natural resources if such measures are made effective in conjunction with restrictions on domestic production or consumption', but only so long as they are 'not applied in a manner which would constitute a means of arbitrary or unjustifiable discrimination between countries where the same conditions prevail, or a disguised restriction on international trade'. There is a body of dispute settlement decisions defining these different terms. These agreements thus frame the ability of the nation state to act in relation to the environment where action falls under the GATT.

Alongside the GATT, the WTO Sanitary and Phytosanitary (SPS) Agreement explicitly requires that all the national regulatory measures of the signatories concerning human, plant, and animal health comply with a series of obligations, so as to ensure that such measures are not barriers to trade. Article 2.2 of the SPS Agreement states that any SPS measure must be 'based on scientific principles' and that it should 'not be maintained without sufficient scientific evidence'. Article 5.1 states:

> Members shall ensure that their sanitary or phytosanitary measures are based on an assessment, as appropriate to the circumstances, of the risks to human, animal or plant life or health, taking into account risk assessment techniques developed by the relevant international organizations.

Each of these legal provisions requires interpretation, and this agreement has also given rise to a series of disputes under the WTO dispute settlement process concerning a range of measures taken by signatory nations. Measures challenged include Australian bans on imported salmon, Japanese bans on imported apples, and EU bans on the use of growth hormones in beef production.

Global environmental law?

The development of international environmental law, as well as the harmonization brought about by global trade, has led some scholars to suggest that what is emerging is 'global environmental law'. Thus, Tseming Yang and Robert Percival argue that these processes have resulted in the development of a common set of 'legal principles and norms' that amount to 'global environmental law'. Others have pointed to the rise of transnational environmental law—a body of environmental law that transcends legal borders.

There is much evidence pointing to common approaches. From one perspective, environmental problems are generic tragedies of the commons. Similar legal approaches have emerged in different jurisdictions—pollution offences, regulatory permitting, and enclave protection in nature conservation. International conventions such as the Rio Declaration have also promoted a core set of environmental law principles and common regulatory approaches such as EIA. Environmental law scholars talk of the 'regulatory diffusion', 'trans-echelon borrowing', and 'uploading' and 'downloading' of different legal and regulatory techniques.

But these commonalities do not mean that nation states and legal cultures disappear. The operation of environmental law is embedded in those legal cultures. Legal culture shapes what is and is not possible. It is also the case that the development of environmental law has not resulted in a tidy overall picture of environmental law. There are multi-level international environmental agreements in some areas, but not others. Even when such agreements exist they do not necessarily strictly bind signatory states, nor result in the same approach being taken in different countries. Climate change is a good example of this—the international regime is largely a framework (Chapter 5), and substantive action in regards to climate change problems is occurring within nation states. The legal and political cultures of nations matter.

Environmental principles are another case in point. They are outlined in the international Rio Declaration, but the case law of each jurisdiction is distinctive. A study of the writing on environmental principles also reveals why a 'global' approach to environmental law is so attractive. As the environmental law scholar Eloise Scotford highlights, global environmental principles are promoted because they are perceived to address both environmental problems *and* legal problems. In regards to the latter, she notes that one of the attractions of principles is that they appear to be 'universal and foundational legal concepts that bring coherence and moral legitimacy to the disorganised, multi-jurisdictional bundle of regulation and decisions that constitute environmental law'. What Scotford is highlighting is that the promotion of global environmental law is driven not just by the reality of commonalities, but also by hopes of making environmental law more rational and more navigable. Given the complexity of both environmental problems and environmental law, that hope is understandable. It is similar to the hope of the non-lawyer that an international treaty will solve an environmental problem (Chapter 3).

Environmental problems do not yield to such simple solutions however. They are problems embedded in the 'imagined communities' of nation states, and even when they transcend those communities the responses to those problems are determined by the legal cultures of nation states.

Chapter 7
Power and accountability in environmental law

One aspect of the role of nation states was not explored in Chapter 6—the power they have over their own citizens. Nation states dominate environmental law because of the need for a comprehensive exercise of authority in response to a collective action problem within any particular jurisdiction. As the political philosopher Robyn Eckersley states, this appeal to the state 'should not be understood as an entirely instrumental appeal'. Rather, 'the state is (potentially) the most *legitimate*, and not just the most powerful social institution'. What makes the exercise of state power legitimate is that it is exercised in accordance with established principles of good government—principles nearly always embodied in law.

Power and freedom

For Hardin, the solution to the tragedy of the commons was the exercise of governmental power. Thus, the solution to the parking problems of East Oxford lay in local government exercising authority. They regulated who could park in the street and enforced the law accordingly. It was that exercise of power that was divisive. Many people did not want their actions regulated and could not see why the state should have this power over them. A similar pattern of perceptions can be seen in Hochschild's work in Louisiana (Chapter 4).

This is not surprising. The need for state intervention to address environmental problems sits uneasily with the meta-narratives of the contemporary era. As the writer Amitav Ghosh argues, much of the modern age has been premised on Enlightenment ideas of individual freedom and action, but 'global warming poses a powerful challenge to the idea that the free pursuit of individual interests always leads to the general good'. The same is true of other environmental problems—hence the tragedies of the commons. All these problems are a physical reminder that our actions impact upon others. It may be a local impact—the emissions from a factory being breathed in by those who live around it; but it may be global—the emissions from cars driven in Germany leading to sea level rises in the Pacific.

Thus questions about 'freedom' are embedded in many disputes over how to respond to environmental problems. Many of those objecting to environmental regulation believe in the importance of unregulated markets and small government. As such, neo-liberal opposition to environmental law is grounded in the opinion that regulation by government is inconsistent with ideas of liberty and free markets.

For example, one of the issues in the 2016 UK referendum on leaving the EU was a perception that the EU was a source of bureaucratic rules—often described as 'regulatory red tape'. In the lead-up to the referendum a number of UK newspapers published articles stating that the EU Commission was postponing regulatory action in relation to the energy efficiency of toasters and kettles. This, they reported, was because such a law would be particularly unattractive given the British love of tea and toast. Three days later the European Commission's Euromyth website made clear they were not planning any such law, and even if they were it would not take the form suggested.

EU laws concerning the ecodesign of home appliances have evolved in a measured and careful way, with scrutiny from the

European Parliament and Council. Around 27 per cent of carbon dioxide emissions are from households and small appliances are often energy intensive. The EU laws have thus, over time and in relation to specific products, introduced a regime, in some cases voluntary, to encourage more energy efficient designs for future products. Besides the cost savings to individual users, and carbon dioxide reductions, such innovation also leads to international competitiveness as energy efficient products have a market edge in global markets. But the detail and the logic largely got lost in reporting. What critics of EU laws emphasized is the way in which environmental laws are an exercise in power over the freedom of individuals.

But just as with the idea of tragedies of the commons, care needs to be taken in not making ideas of freedom too reductionist. Freedom can mean many different things, and 'free will' has little meaning if societies live in environmental misery. As Eckersley has argued, the role of the state is often about ensuring 'the ecological freedom of its citizens'. Commitments to environmental protection also operate right across the political spectrum. Thus, embedded in traditional ideas of conservatism are commitments to environmental stewardship.

What all these examples highlight is that behind many environmental debates and disagreements are disagreements about the power of the state. Some disagreements are in the realm of polemics, some in the realm of philosophy. Some disagreements are heartfelt and some are generated for political gain. These disagreements are a reminder that perceptions about what constitutes a good and legitimate nation state shape perceptions about what is an environmental problem.

Mary Douglas, one of the great anthropologists of the 20th century, explored how pollution is something that is deemed to be out of place and not normal. As she noted, writing with the political scientist Aaron Wildavsky, 'it implies an abnormal intrusion of foreign elements'. Ideas of abnormality and foreignness, however, depend on a theory of what is normal, and those theories interrelate with understandings of how society does, and should operate. Beliefs in free markets go hand in hand with a belief in a robust environment that does not require special legal protection—if markets can bounce back, so can nature. It is thus not surprising that a number of libertarians doubt the anthropocentric causes of climate change. In contrast, conservative ideas of environmental stewardship often operate in tandem with ideas of social stewardship.

None of this is to say that environmental problems are not real. What it does highlight is that, as we saw in Chapter 2, bound up in environmental problems are questions about the power of the state and what is a 'good society'. Ensuring the exercise of legitimate state power is not simply a functional task, but one that invokes a whole range of prescriptions about what states should do.

The need for public administration

In exercising its power in relation to environmental problems, the state cannot remain an abstract entity. Power is exercised through its institutional architecture. Environmental law creates all sorts of new governing rules. It makes it an offence to pollute. Trade in endangered species is banned. A permit must be obtained to carry out an activity. If these laws are breached there are consequences. A fine may be levied or in extreme cases someone could go to jail.

The history of environmental law has shown that the enacting of new rules was never enough to ensure compliance and/or to achieve a legislature's objective. Environmental problems required the creation of new public institutions, particularly administrative institutions. This is because the other arms of government—legislatures and courts—did not have the capacity to administer environmental law. The creation, application, and enforcement of environmental law is resource intensive. It needs information collection, analysis, and assessment. Prescriptions about environmental quality need to be applied to specific situations. 'A high level of protection' needs to be translated into an actual applicable standard in light of the information available. Discussions need to occur to integrate information and insights from different perspectives. Expertise is needed to bring all these things together. Moreover, that expertise needs to be ongoing. As scientific knowledge changes, environmental laws need to be revised.

The administrative institutions of environmental law take many different forms, including central government departments, independent regulatory agencies, scientific advisors, and committees. Environmental legislation, as passed by legislatures, thus tends to provide a framework for action, and these different administrative agencies then pass delegated legislation or make individual decisions in accordance with that framework. The administrative nature of environmental law is seen at all levels within a nation. Scholars have also argued that the institutions seen at the international level (Chapter 5), such as the UNEP and the organizational structures connected to the UNFCCC, are also administrative in nature.

Accountability and administrative law

The administrative reality of environmental law creates a paradox. A commitment to environmental quality is a feature of advanced democracies, but that commitment requires vesting power in unelected administrative institutions. This is where the role of law, specifically administrative law, becomes so significant. Administrative law is concerned with constituting, limiting, and holding public administration to account to ensure administrative power is legitimately exercised. It does so in many ways, including creating rules for how delegated legislation should be passed, rules concerning freedom of information, and rules about the conduct of public officials and accountability processes.

Anne Davies, a leading public law scholar, divides accountability processes into four steps: the setting of 'yardsticks' against which an account will be judged; the obtaining of an account; the judging of an account; and taking action in light of that judgment. The first of these steps involves the determination of what public administration ought to do and how it ought to do it. It raises issues about power and freedom, and it is a subject that people within a political community may disagree on. Davies' other steps highlight that accountability processes can take many forms. Accountability processes can be committees of inquiry, forms of regulatory impact assessment, or some other form of regulatory oversight.

Lawyers place much emphasis on the role of the courts in holding public administration to account. Courts, through a process called judicial review, oversee administrative decision-making to ensure it is within the power granted to an administrative decision-maker. Many environmental law cases, including *Massachusetts v EPA* (Chapter 3), *Sierra Club v Morton* (Chapter 5), and *Rapanos v US* (Chapter 6), are judicial review cases. The emphasis placed on courts by administrative law scholars is another example of the emphasis placed on legal stability. Courts, in judicially reviewing decision-making, are holding administrative decision-makers to account by assessing the legal validity of an administrative decision in relation to existing legal doctrines and principles. This is because, as Latour argued after conducting an ethnography of French administrative law courts, lawyers 'even when they make an especially daring argument for overturning established precedents have to secure the integrity of the legal edifice, continuity in the exercise of power, and smoothness in the application of the law'. The quality of the judgment lies in this process of reasoning, and judicial review results in a judgment in which that reasoning can be scrutinized.

Much of the complexity and technical detail of environmental law comes from its administrative law nature. The nature of administrative law doctrine does vary from legal culture to legal culture, but in each legal system there is a large body of case law concerning how a court determines these questions. Those legal questions will come in many different shapes and forms. They may involve questions about the correct legal interpretation of a statute, or they may involve questions about whether administrative power was exercised fairly and reasonably. In all cases, a court adjudicates on these issues in accordance with administrative law doctrine.

Legal cultures shape administrative power in quite dramatic ways. Thus for example, the Fifth Amendment of the US Constitution states that private property shall not 'be taken for public use, without just compensation'. Many legal cases have been brought in which property owners have argued that environmental regulations, such as endangered species legislation or laws preventing coastal development to stop coastal erosion, have effectively resulted in their property being 'taken' because they have reduced the value of that property and/or limited the use to which it can be put. The answer in these cases is rarely 'yes, that is taking' or 'no, that is not taking'. Rather, these cases involve the application of a series of nuanced doctrines that define what 'taking' means in a range of different circumstances. In contrast, in the UK the absence of an equivalent constitutional guarantee means that the legal issue of 'taking' in environmental law has a low profile, and thus the role of property rights has also been less prominent. The powers of decision-makers in the US and the UK are thus being shaped and limited by different legal doctrines.

Science

The need for expertise, and particularly scientific expertise, is one of the justifications for the central role that public administration plays in environmental law. Scientific analysis allows environmental problems to be identified and aids in the development of effective responses to those problems. Physics, chemistry, biology (including ecology), and interdisciplinary scientific fields such as meteorology and the medical sciences are all relevant to environmental problems. The work in these different areas also covers a vast swathe of disciplinary practices, ranging from purely theoretical scientific research to applied research, environmental monitoring, and what Sheila Jasanoff has described as 'regulatory science': the production and synthesis of information with a particular emphasis on making predictions.

Science also contributes to the legitimacy of administrative action. A decision based on the facts is more likely to be consistent with the rule of law than one that is not. As the historian Theodore Porter has pointed out, 'scientific objectivity...provides an answer to a moral demand for impartiality and fairness'. In this way, science, as Jasanoff notes, 'exercises constitutive power in the modern world, enabling and constraining the actions of states and citizens as legal constitutions do'.

Science is thus fundamental to environmental law. But the limits of science mean that there are often genuine disagreements over whether there is enough scientific information on which to act, and even if that information exists, what action should be taken. These disagreements occur among scientists and non-scientists. They are also entangled with questions about the legitimacy of state power.

The importance of, and limits of, science is why the precautionary principle, commonly identified as one of the core environmental principles, has been so popular and so controversial. That principle comes in many variations, but generally states that in cases where there is a threat of serious environmental damage 'lack of full scientific certainty' should not be a basis for not taking action to prevent such damage. Proponents of the principle point to a long history of regulatory decisions being delayed until too late because regulators were forced to wait until full proof of harm was established. The delayed regulation of asbestos and tobacco products are two prime examples. Critics of the principle fear that it gives too much power to states to exercise coercive power on the basis of speculation and guesswork.

The role of science in environmental law is not only about the application of the precautionary principle. Empowering and limiting the scientific aspect of administrative institutions is an important aspect of creating these institutions and regulating their power. In Victorian England, scientific expertise was primarily deployed through inspectors, whose task was to enforce pollution laws. In contrast, in the US in the early 1970s the EPA was created by a bipartisan Congress with a significant institutional capacity to carry out regulatory science. Article 191(3) of the TFEU requires EU institutions to take account of 'available scientific and technical data' in preparing policy on the environment. The designation of a species as 'endangered' or 'threatened' under the US Endangered Species Act 1973 (ESA) requires that a number of factual determinations are made. Administrative frameworks such as risk assessment and regulatory impact assessment regulate the factual inquiries of decision-makers.

More significantly, ensuring there is a proper scientific basis to a decision is often a focus of accountability processes. As Lord Justice Beatson noted in the case of *Mott v Environment Agency* (2016):

> A reviewing court needs to be given a sufficient explanation by a regulator operating in a technical or scientific area of how the science relates to its decision so that the court can consider whether it embodies an abuse of discretion or an error of law.

As such, he found it was the 'duty of such a body to assist the court with full and accurate explanations of all the facts relevant to the issue the court must decide'. Therein lies a challenge. Administrative lawyers rarely have the relevant scientific training for the scientific issues they encounter. A preoccupation of environmental law is thus managing this challenge.

Judicial review in action

Alongside that preoccupation are many others—all concerned with whether administrative decision-makers have stayed within the power granted by legislation and have exercised that power fairly and properly. These questions are legal questions, but the answers are not always settled legally. It is also the case that courts in judicial review police the power of administration and do not substitute their discretionary judgment for that of the administrative decision-maker. To make matters more complicated, administrative law is operating in a politicized context. While law is not politics, different normative assumptions about the role of the state and about the nature of administrative expertise translate into different assumptions about the legal power of environmental decision-makers. Accountability processes thus become forums for deciding questions of law and for contesting visions of good public administration.

This was seen in *Rapanos v US* (Chapter 6) and can also be seen in the US Supreme Court case of *Environmental Protection Agency v EME Homer City Generation* (2012). It is one of the many judicial review challenges brought against the US EPA in relation to power they have exercised under the Clean Air Act. Under that act the EPA sets national air quality standards, and states must implement those standards through their own implementation plans. As part of this multi-level regime the EPA must sign off on each state's plans, and in doing so ensures that the plan complies with what is known as the Good Neighbour Provision. This requires plans to 'contain adequate provisions' that prohibit 'any source or other type of emissions activity within the State from emitting any air pollutant in amounts which will... contribute significantly to nonattainment in, or interfere with maintenance by, any other State'. The provision addresses the

7. Industrial smoke stacks in Florida.

problem of emissions (Figure 7) in an upwind state adversely
impacting the air quality in a downwind state.

The EPA interpreted this provision to take into account the cost of
abatement of certain emissions activity in an upwind state. The
result was that the Good Neighbour Provision would only apply to
upwind state emissions which were cost effective to abate. The
question for the Supreme Court was whether the Clean Air Act's
statutory framework permitted the EPA to exercise its
interpretative power in this way.

The majority in the Supreme Court said it did. Justice Ginsburg,
writing for the majority, noted:

> For several reasons, curtailing interstate air pollution poses a
> complex challenge for environmental regulators. First, identifying
> the upwind origin of downwind air pollution is no easy endeavour.
> Most upwind States propel pollutants to more than one downwind
> State, many downwind States receive pollution from multiple
> upwind States, and some States qualify as both upwind and

downwind…. The overlapping and interwoven linkages between upwind and downwind States with which EPA had to contend number in the thousands.

Given these complexities, Justice Ginsburg saw the role of the EPA as 'crafting a solution' to a 'thorny causation problem', and thus the EPA could not take a quantitative and proportional approach to assessing the issue of contribution. The agency could take into account abatement costs in trying to draw a line between under- and overregulation. Thus, Justice Ginsburg noted:

> Eliminating those amounts that can cost-effectively be reduced is an efficient and equitable solution to the allocation problem the Good Neighbour Provision requires the Agency to address. Efficient because EPA can achieve the levels of attainment, i.e., of emission reductions, the proportional approach aims to achieve, but at a much lower overall cost. Equitable because, by imposing uniform cost thresholds on regulated States, EPA's rule subjects to stricter regulation those States that have done relatively less in the past to control their pollution. Upwind States that have not yet implemented pollution controls of the same stringency as their neighbours will be stopped from free riding on their neighbours' efforts to reduce pollution. They will have to bring down their emissions by installing devices of the kind in which neighbouring States have already invested.

The court resolved the legal question about the limits of the EPA's power by reference to the nature of the environmental problem being dealt with and the role of the EPA in dealing with it.

Justice Scalia took a different approach, grounded in different understandings of the problem and the powers of the EPA. In his first line he stated: 'Too many important decisions of the Federal Government are made nowadays by unelected agency officials exercising broad lawmaking authority, rather than by the people's representatives in Congress.' From this perspective, he thought it desirable that legislation be understood as the 'source and ceiling' of EPA authority. Thus for Justice Scalia:

> The statute addresses solely the environmental consequences of emissions, *not* the facility of reducing them; and it requires States to shoulder burdens in proportion to the size of their contributions, not in proportion to the ease of bearing them.

Moreover, for Justice Scalia the EPA's task was largely one of quantitative assessment, managed through a technical process of assessment. Thus, he noted:

> I fully acknowledge that the proportional-reduction approach will demand some complicated computations where one upwind State is linked to multiple downwind States and vice versa. I am confident, however, that EPA's skilled number-crunchers can adhere to the statute's *quantitative* (rather than efficiency) mandate by crafting quantitative solutions.

What can be seen in both judgments is how legal questions are intertwined with questions about the nature of legitimate expert administrative power. Justice Scalia wanted agency officials to do no more than technical 'number crunching', while Justice Ginsburg was more comfortable with the EPA crafting 'efficient' and 'equitable' solutions.

Turn to other jurisdictions and the importance of law in regulating power in the environmental law context can also be seen. Many of the most significant administrative law and constitutional law cases of the last twenty-five years have been environmental cases. The legal questions in each legal culture are different, but often turn on subtle and contentious issues.

Take, for example, a recent legal debate over the interpretation of the principles set out in New Zealand's Resource Management Act 1991. Over time, the New Zealand courts interpreted the principles to require an 'overall judgment' approach on the part of the decision-maker. This was because, as one judge noted, the act has 'a deliberate openness about the language, its meanings and its connotations'. The 'overall judgment' approach meant that the application of the principles would be legally assessed in the round. This approach brings with it the danger that reasoning can be opaque and not easily assessed. In *Environmental Defence Society Incorporated v The New Zealand King Salmon Company Ltd* (2014), the New Zealand Supreme Court stated:

> A danger of the 'overall judgment' approach is that decision-makers may conclude too readily that there is a conflict between particular policies and prefer one over another, rather than making a thoroughgoing attempt to find a way to reconcile them.

They thus proposed another approach which required a more explicit reasoning process.

Environmental law is not just about responding to environmental problems, but ensuring that institutional responses to such problems are legitimate, accountable, and within the powers granted to public administration. As these cases attest, this is not a straightforward exercise. As the US administrative law scholar Louis Jaffe stated, administrative power 'has in it the inherent power to hurt, to awaken resentment, to stir the sense of injustice'. In doing so it raises a series of legal, political, and philosophical questions about the legitimacy of state power.

Chapter 8
Ensuring the effectiveness of environmental law

In exploring environmental law, the primary focus so far has been on its internal reasoning: the words of a legislative scheme, the legal concepts that lawyers sculpt, and the institutions that law creates. But the experience in many jurisdictions is that law on the books does not always translate into law in action. It doesn't matter how beautifully constructed a statute is, if pollution continues to pour into a river that the statute intends to protect then the law is a failure.

Assessing success

Much of the stretching of the legal imagination of environmental lawyers has thus been in terms of trying to make environmental law more effective. Enforcement practices have evolved, innovative regulatory strategies have been developed, and courts have been entrusted with a role in enforcement. Care needs to be taken in thinking about effectiveness however. In particular, to assess the accomplishments of environmental law, the complexity of environmental problems cannot be ignored.

There are many examples of environmental law success stories—the Montreal Protocol on Substances that Deplete the Ozone Layer 1987 and the UK Clean Air Act 1956 are examples where serious problems were addressed by specific laws. Controlling parking in my street transformed that street overnight. The legal protection of species in the US considerably reduces the likelihood of them becoming extinct. But the success of many other environmental laws is less obvious. Environmental quality is improved incrementally over time. Environmental benefits are experienced by future generations. Environmental disasters are averted, but there is nothing to show that it was the law that made the difference. Likewise, in regards to an issue such as climate change, success is also about developing greater resilience within societies for them to adapt to, and manage, the physical impacts of climate change.

The effective management of environmental problems is also an ongoing process. Air quality must continue to be monitored and emissions regulated. Species cannot be protected one year and not the next. Regulation needs to be comprehensive. Ignoring one set of significant causes of an environmental problem while regulating another less significant set will not improve environmental quality. The successes of environmental law are thus highly dependent on the ongoing management of the detail—the careful consideration of each regulatory permit, the revision and refinement of air quality standards, the conscientious determination of emission targets—none of which can be easily spun into glamorous headlines about environmental protection victories.

As explored in Chapter 7, the successes of environmental law must also be legitimate. The exercise of power pursuant to an environmental statute must be legally valid, as must the methods by which disputes that arise concerning the operation of environmental laws are resolved. To use the words of the political theorist Jürgen Habermas, legitimacy is about the 'worthiness to be recognised'. That worthiness is dependent on the consistency of environmental law with established principles of good government, not about whether everyone is happy with the outcome.

The controversies of success

Therein lies a challenge. Determining what is legitimate success is difficult given the controversies over environmental problems and their management. In light of the different ecocentric and anthropocentric values placed on environmental protection (Chapter 2), it is unlikely that all will be satisfied with the results of a particular environmental protection measure. For example, in the US the listing of polar bears as 'threatened' under the ESA in 2008 was challenged by industry associations as overly protective, and by environmental organizations as not protective enough.

The successes of environmental protection may also not figure in a world view. In 1978 the US Supreme Court in *Tennessee Valley Authority v Hill* granted an injunction stopping the completion of a dam because it would have violated the ESA by jeopardizing the continued existence of a listed endangered species—the snail darter fish (Figure 8). The eminent legal theorist Ronald Dworkin noted about the case that:

> The conservationists discovered that one almost finished TVA dam, costing over one hundred million dollars, would be likely to destroy the only habitat of the snail darter, a three-inch fish of no particular beauty or biological interest or general ecological importance.

But for conservationists the fish did not need to have these features to be worthy of legal protection.

The US legal scholar Richard Epstein has struggled with the way the ESA interacts with property rights. The 'taking' of threatened and endangered species under the legislation was interpreted by the US Supreme Court in another case to include 'significant habit modification or degradation where it actually kills or injures wildlife'. Epstein found this interpretation

8. Snail darter fish.

problematic: 'Our property baselines have to be defined, as they have always been defined, to make the necessity for legal intervention the exception not the rule.' For him the starting point for legal analysis was the 'well understood system of property rights', and for him the court's interpretation cut across those rights. On the other hand, destroying the habitat of an endangered species is sure to harm it and thus to effectively 'take' it. To ignore that fact would be to undercut the purpose behind the ESA.

The successes of environmental law will thus often be contested. Addressing environmental problems also raises questions about what are 'fair' successes. Curbing pollution may lead to increased production costs and thus the increased cost of a product. Banning a product may lead to some consumer items no longer being available on the market. And some of the choices to be made are between two environmental goods. Hydroelectric dams are reliable sources of renewable electricity, but the building of them requires flooding areas and this leads to the displacement of people and the destruction of wilderness.

In some cases, a compromise can be found between these different views and these different values. Pollution control is an example where emissions can be limited and economic growth can be preserved. Many studies have shown that strict pollution laws lead to technological innovation and new economic opportunities. A central tenet of EU environmental policy is that the EU's environmental leadership leads to international economic competitiveness. In these cases, policymakers talk of 'win–win' solutions in which improved environmental quality leads to economic growth and greater profits. Thus the European Commission emphasizes the importance of enforcing environmental law so that '[s]trict enforcement also stimulates the market to find innovative ways to increase resource efficiency and reduce import dependency'.

But in some cases, a compromise cannot be found and there are winners and losers. If forest wilderness is logged the forestry company makes a profit, its shareholders are paid dividends, and people can buy the timber. But the wilderness and its ecosystem are lost. If the forest is not logged, they are maintained, but at the cost of losing the other gains. The long-term benefits of environmental protection measures are also often invisible to those who have lost out. Ultimately a decision has to be made between competing visions of the environment and how we live in it. By enforcing residents' only parking in my street, the local authority favoured the interests of residents over the interests of commuters, shoppers, and traders. None of this is to say that environmental law and its effectiveness are not important. The point is that success is not a simple ideal. The successes of environmental law will also be assessed against other values.

The challenges of enforcement

The successes of environmental law are contested and hard fought. Success also requires proper enforcement. As the legal scholar Carolyn Abbot notes, 'it is the enforcement process which puts the flesh on the bones of any regulatory system'. The problem is that the proper implementation of environmental law is often put in the 'too difficult' basket. Take air quality standards. In many cities across the world, the local standards set for air quality are not met. This is because enforcing those standards often requires widespread change—for example, the banning of particular types of vehicles or even dramatically reducing traffic in a city. The economic and political will is often not present. Thus, in the EU proper implementation of environmental directives has long been a problem. Similar issues can be seen in other jurisdictions, particularly when the enforcement of environmental laws is perceived as getting in the way of economic progress. Perceived, because ultimately such progress will be undercut by poor environmental quality.

Enforcement also requires resources, a fact that also contributes to a lack of political will to deliver environmental law. Staff are needed to enforce a law, and they also need to detect breaches of the law. A breach of a law may go undetected. The illegal dumping of waste is unlikely to occur in broad daylight and in full view. The breach of an environmental law may also occur on private property. Laws against land clearing in Australia have often been difficult to enforce for this reason. Technologies such as satellite imagery and pollution monitors can assist in the enforcement process, but these also require further resources. If a breach of the law is detected, an enforcement body needs to prosecute in accordance with the laws of a legal system so as to ensure any enforcement is fair. This can be a lengthy process that requires professional legal advice and the careful collation and presentation of evidence to a court.

Enforcement practices vary significantly between legal cultures. In England there is a long tradition, dating back to the Victorian era, of only using prosecution as a last resort. Pollution enforcement officers thus saw their role as aiding those who were being regulated to comply with the law. In more recent times, the Environment Agency in that jurisdiction has an 'Enforcement and Sanctions

Statement'. Its overall philosophy is 'to engage with business to educate and enable compliance' by encouraging 'individuals and businesses to put the environment first and to integrate good environmental practices into normal working methods'. This 'risk based' approach to enforcement is admirable, but can be inadequate in the face of determined, bad-faith non-compliance or complete incompetence on the part of those being regulated. In other jurisdictions, such as the US, enforcement is a less consultative affair and far more formalized. These differences reflect distinct legal and socio-political cultures (Chapter 6).

Engaging the public

Given all this it is not surprising that a major feature of environmental law is the development of legal and regulatory techniques to make environmental law more effective and enforceable. One set of ways of doing this has been to engage the public through vesting in them a range of different rights to participate and enforce environmental laws.

Thus, one of the purposes of the public participation and information rights contained in the Aarhus Convention (Chapter 4) is to promote the effectiveness of environmental law. Such rights promote awareness about environmental quality, provide decision-makers with information about local environmental conditions and/or the public's value preferences about the environment, and promote accountability. Public participation is thus understood to increase the problem-solving capacity of decision-makers, which in turn improves the effectiveness of environmental solutions.

The Aarhus Convention is simply one example of public participation and information being used to make environmental law more effective. Environmental statutes often have provisions requiring administrative decision-makers to consult with the public as well as setting out the basis on which decisions will be made.

Likewise, access to information laws often have as their purpose the promoting of public participation and ensuring that the public can assess for themselves the basis of decision-making. Alongside these legislative provisions, many administrative institutions have developed administrative practices to increase public participation.

The varied nature of different participation and environmental information obligations has raised questions among scholars about their genuine nature. In the 1970s, Sherry Arnstein described a ladder of citizen participation. At the bottom was public participation as tokenism and at the top were forms of public participation in which stakeholders were truly empowered. Public participation can also be hindered by the expertise or resources needed to comment on a decision properly. This is particularly true when there is a range of technical reports accompanying a decision that are not easily understandable by the general public.

Alongside participation rights, environmental legislation often gives rights to the public to enforce the law in a courtroom. This is a common feature of statutes in the US. The expansion of standing discussed in Chapter 5 has also enabled the more effective enforcement of environmental law by allowing a wider range of people to bring legal actions.

In all these contexts, the 'public' can mean many different things. It can refer to general members of the public and environmental organizations, but also to economic actors. Thus, in the English case of *Ardagh Glass Ltd v Chester City Council* (2009), a glass company brought a legal action to require a local planning authority to enforce planning law against a competitor glass company that had not got proper planning permission for building the 'largest glass container factory in Europe'. The logic behind such an action is understandable—by not complying with the law the competitor company gained an unfair advantage in the glass container marketplace.

There is a temptation to see the public as a wellspring of civic virtue, and as such a solution to the challenges of enforcement, but the role of the public is nuanced and multifaceted. Members of the public often have entrenched views about environmental protection, views that don't sit easily with the complexity of environmental problems. Likewise, particularly in the US, there have been examples of significant economic interests creating environmental groups that promote their own economic interests in a practice colloquially known as 'astroturfing'. None of this is to discount the important role of the public. It is another reminder that there are no simple solutions in environmental law.

Reflexive environmental law

One example of the way in which public participation is inherent in the pursuit of effective environmental law is the logic of EIA (see Chapter 5). While EIA regimes vary between different jurisdictions, nearly all EIA laws require a decision-maker to analyse environmental impacts *and* consult the public. Lord Hoffmann, of the UK House of Lords, noted in *Berkeley v Secretary of State for the Environment* (2000):

> The [EU EIA] Directive requires not merely that the planning authority should have the necessary information, but that it should have been obtained by means of a particular procedure, namely that of an EIA. And an essential element in this procedure is that what the Regulations call the 'environmental statement' by the developer should have been 'made available to the public' and that the public should have been 'given the opportunity to express an opinion' in accordance with article 6(2) of the Directive.

The role of the public is thus understood to enhance the effectiveness of the EIA process. The public can scrutinize an environmental statement and review it for its accuracy and robustness. Lord Hoffmann's statement was not just an observation. Interpreting the directive in this way meant that the court needed to ensure that a decision-maker had substantially complied with both elements of the process.

EIA also represents the development of an innovative regulatory technique that addresses the problems of enforcement not just through involving the public, but also in changing the mindset of decision-makers. One of the purposes of EIA is to encourage decision-makers to take the environmental impacts of a project into account early in decision-making, thus preventing the need to regulate adverse environmental impacts later in the process.

Legal scholars thus describe EIA as 'reflexive'—it forces both public and private decision-makers to internalize environmental concerns into their management cultures. Strategic environmental assessment (SEA) is an even more radical version of such reflexivity. It requires decision-makers not just to think about environmental protection in relation to specific decisions, but to incorporate it into the process of developing strategies and policies.

The reflexive logic of EIA does pose a conundrum for assessing its success. The true success of EIA would be that no project would ever require an EIA because projects would be designed so that they were not likely to have a significant effect on the environment. A lack of EIAs, however, may also represent a failure of legal implementation of an EIA regime.

Similar problems with assessing the successes of reflexive environmental laws can be seen in other areas. In England and Wales the contaminated land liability regime is seen as a 'last resort'. The regulatory logic is that contaminated land should be cleaned up as part of the planning process, as developers will have economic incentives to do this as a precondition to gaining planning permission. But does this mean the very small number of cases which have been brought for contaminated land liability is due to the success of the planning system, or rather just due to poor enforcement? It is difficult to know.

Regulatory innovation and pollution control

From one perspective, the problems of effective environmental law are due to poor legal design. This thinking can be seen in relation to pollution control. Traditional pollution laws take the form of command and control laws. The law sets out a rule or a standard (the command) and if that is breached then the law is enforced (the control). Command and control regulation can take many forms, including emissions standards and technology standards. As the US environmental law scholar Carol Rose notes, command and control laws are based on a 'RIGHTWAY' logic. The command sets out the right way 'in which [a] resource is used or taken, effectively prescribing the methods by which users may take the resource'. The problem with a RIGHTWAY logic is that it limits action to what is included in the command, and does not encourage other approaches to addressing environmental problems.

Since the 1990s many jurisdictions have developed other regulatory strategies in relation to pollution control. Some of these have directly addressed the issue of enforcement. For example, Ian Ayres and John Braithwaite's idea of 'responsive regulation' aims to focus enforcement practices where they are most needed. This might seem similar to the practices in the UK, but responsive regulation takes this further by taking into account organizational structures of both regulators and the regulated. It thus overlaps with ideas of reflexive law, and also ideas of self-regulation. Another approach, seen in limited contexts in the US and the EU, has been the development of individual agreements with specific industries to address environmental issues.

There are also examples where different forms of liability are created to address environmental problems. In Brazil, 'collective moral damages' can be awarded by a court in environmental cases to provide a fund for addressing ongoing environmental problems.

In the EU, there is an Environmental Liability Directive that requires polluters to compensate for environmental harm in certain circumstances.

Most of these reforms focus on the control aspect of command and control. Another front of regulatory innovation has been the reimagining of commands. For example, pollution laws have been reconfigured around environmental quality standards. In the EU, water quality laws were completely transformed in 2000 so that their focus is now on the 'good ecological status' of river basins rather than on prescribing emission standards. This shift in regulatory thinking is dramatic. It has required the creation of new institutions (often operating across national boundaries) and a range of regulatory processes for determining what 'good ecological status' is, and what the implications of it are for activity in a specific river basin.

Markets

Much of the regulatory innovation of the last three decades has used the power of the market. This is another solution to the tragedy of the commons. Rather than regulate it, the remedy is to privatize the commons so that it no longer exists and therefore no tragedy can arise. Thus, in relation to greenhouse gases, Article 17 of the Kyoto Protocol encourages the use of emission trading schemes. These schemes effectively privatize the commons and transforms it into a tradable commodity. Polluters are allocated pollution credits that allow them to pollute a certain amount, and if they don't use these credits they can sell them on. In many schemes, the number of credits allocated reduce over time. The simple logic of these schemes is that operators have an economic incentive to reduce pollution.

Ecolabelling laws and certification schemes use the power of the market in a different way. They require information to be given to potential customers about the environmental aspects of a product—whether it is energy efficient, whether it has been produced in a sustainable way, and so on. Consumers will then use their market power and make buying choices that are more environmentally friendly. An excellent example of this is the EU chemicals law known as REACH. Article 5 states 'no data, no market', and the law requires that all chemicals sold or imported into the EU are accompanied with data about their environmental and health risks. The logic of the law is that those buying chemicals will naturally prefer chemicals that present fewer risks.

It is tempting to see the development of these market regulatory techniques in superficial terms as law simply harnessing the invisible hand of the market. But as the legal scholar Sanja Bogojević has shown in relation to emission trading schemes, any such scheme will create a market on a particular logic and simultaneously constitute the power of the state in a particular way. Thus, she argues, such schemes can be just a variation on a command and control scheme or a more radical vesting of pollution property rights in private hands. To put the matter another way, issues about power and framing the world do not disappear with the deployment of these techniques. Nor do legal disputes, due to the fact that these schemes raise many of the legal questions we see in other areas of environmental law, particularly questions concerning power and accountability.

Courts and enforcement

Courts have also played an important role in enforcement. That role is not on the initiative of judges. Cases need to be brought to courts by litigants and that is why the expansion of standing has been an important aspect of ensuring the effectiveness of environmental law.

For example, courts in the UK, India, Argentina, and Pakistan have enforced the law in cases where the momentum for enforcement has been lacking. In 2015, the UK Supreme Court made a mandatory order to compel the UK government to comply with the EU Air Quality Directive. The order was issued a week before a national election and the court stated: 'The new Government, whatever its political complexion, should be left in no doubt as to the need for immediate action to address this issue.' The Indian Supreme Court has, over many years, developed a rich body of enforcement law which has even included ordering the creation of new public bodies to address pollution problems.

Over several years, the Argentinian courts, through the issuing of a series of complex remedies, oversaw the clean-up of the heavily polluted Matanza Riachuelo River Basin (Figure 9). As the Chief Justice of Argentina notes, this was an ongoing, 'deliberative process where the political authorities were forced to make their decisions after an ample process of collective discussion which included public hearings'. Critics argue that courts in these instances are overreaching and engaging in judicial activism. But in many of these cases the courts enforce laws that exist, and in so doing uphold the rule of law.

9. Pollution on the Riachuelo River, Argentina.

Beyond this, courts also contribute to securing the effectiveness of environmental law through providing authoritative interpretations of the law and adjudicating disputes. The courts thus contribute to legal certainty and legal stability. This is not only in relation to conventional command and control law, but also innovative regulatory techniques. The EU emission trading scheme has been heavily litigated. The Environmental Liability Directive has given rise to questions about who are the relevant polluters under the directive and what environmental damage are they liable for. There are thousands of cases about EIA and SEA. None of this is surprising: the pursuit of effective environmental law is also the pursuit of a legitimate and authoritative body of law. Regulatory innovation does not make the complexities and uncertainties of the subject go away. Effectiveness is important, but a multidimensional ideal.

Chapter 9
The many forms of environmental justice

For many lawyers and non-lawyers alike environmental law is, and should be, about justice. The socio-political complexity of environmental problems means, however, that justice in the environmental law context is not a single ideal. It is many songlines, many ways of forging meaning, which cross and intersect across the landscape of environmental law. Some of these practices are the songlines of mainstream legal cultures, some are not.

The songlines of environmental justice wind their way from the local context of the neighbourhood dispute to the global level where they are expressed in international conventions such as the Aarhus Convention (Chapter 4). They also cross over into aspiration. The desire for environmental justice also pervades the relationships between nations and the relationships embedded in globalization. There are also more radical desires for law to be grounded in an Earth jurisprudence, and thus for law to be entirely reconfigured.

The environmental rule of law

The traditional ideal of justice in Western legal thought is Justitia—a blindfolded woman holding a sword and scales. Many variations of her have existed over the centuries. The emphasis on legal stability, fairness, and the resolution of legal disputes by the application of robust legal reasoning all reflect this idea of justice. The proper operation of the courts is also a practical manifestation of Justitia. Courts do many things: they interpret and apply the law, they attribute responsibility and determine liability, they hold decision-makers to account, they ensure that laws and other forms of binding agreements are implemented, and they delineate the boundaries of lawful, executive action. As seen throughout this book, all these issues arise in the operation of environmental law.

In doing all these things the courts are resolving disputes that 'honeycomb' environmental problems. They do so with a commitment to the rule of law and legal stability. The adjudication of disputes serves both a practical purpose in resolving disputes and also a wider, more expository role in declaring what the law is. Courts provide authoritative determinations of what it means to be responsible, what is required to determine causation, and what the upholding of a legal right entails. Court cases contribute to legal stability and to the process of integrating environmental law into the 'seamless web of the law'.

Given this it is not surprising that UNEP stresses the importance of the 'environmental rule of law'—that is, a commitment to uphold and enforce existing laws and to ensure adequate and independent forums of judicial dispute resolution. The first of these issues was discussed in Chapter 8. The second issue is reflected in the fact that an important aspect of environmental law reform has been the redesign of court processes to increase the capacity of courts to consider environmental law disputes.

Capacity building is important because the nature of environmental problems has meant that there have been barriers to courts hearing and adjudicating disputes about them. The most obvious barriers concern access to courts, and have arisen because many legal systems require those wanting to litigate to have individual rights that they are seeking to protect by such litigation. Environmental problems affect many people, and in doing so the disputes they give rise to are frequently not disputes over individual rights. Thus, as we saw in Chapter 5, modification of the laws of standing is required to address this problem. Alongside these developments, there has also been an emphasis on ensuring that there are no other barriers to environmental law cases being brought to court.

For example, the Aarhus Convention requires that access to courts is not 'prohibitively expensive'. Most litigation brought by private parties has an economic aspect—compensation, the protection of property rights, the enforcement of a contract. That economic aspect is missing in many environmental law cases. Litigants bring actions to uphold the law or to protect the environment, not to make an economic gain. The costs of litigation cannot be offset against potential economic rewards, and thus such costs are a barrier to the environmental rule of law. This is particularly true in jurisdictions, such as the UK, where the losing party usually pays the winning party's legal costs. Not only are there no economic gains from winning, but there are serious economic losses from losing. As such, in light of the Aarhus Convention this rule has been adapted in England and Wales for environmental judicial review challenges against the government. It is another example of a legal order having to adapt to take into account environmental problems and environmental law.

But access to the courts has not been the only issue. Capacity building also concerns the substance of what courts do. Most significantly, environmental law reform has focused on the creation of courts and tribunals that are specially tailored to hear and adjudicate environmental law disputes. The most established of these is the New South Wales Land and Environment Court (NSWLEC) in Australia, and there are now over 350 specialized courts and tribunals across the world. Each court or tribunal has a distinct set of powers and operates in a different place in the judicial hierarchy of a legal culture.

One of the perceived strengths of such courts and tribunals is their expertise. That expertise has two aspects. The first is expertise in environmental law. The complexities of environmental legislation mean that having judges with experience and knowledge of the area ensures the robust resolution of legal disputes. The second aspect of expertise is in regards to understanding environmental problems. Thus, the NSWLEC offers a range of different dispute resolution mechanisms apart from adjudication, including conciliation and mediation. It has also developed evidential procedures which allow for a more thorough exploration of the factual issues. This includes experts giving their evidence at the same time, rather than sequentially—a process colloquially known as 'hot-tubbing'.

In all these cases the pursuit of environmental justice is not the simple pursuit of an abstract ideal. It is about engagement with the legal detail of institutions and processes. Like enforcement (Chapter 8) it also requires resources.

Environmental democracy

Overlapping with ideals of the environmental rule of law are ideals of environmental democracy. The Aarhus Convention not only provides for access to justice, but also access to environmental information and public participation. These were discussed in Chapter 8 in terms of what they contribute to the effectiveness of environmental law, but it is important to note that they also have a more substantive aspect. For many scholars, information and public participation are required so as to foster environmental democracy.

Environmental democracy can take many forms, and it can be both ecocentric and anthropocentric in nature (Chapter 2). Generally speaking, it involves a wide number of people being involved in decision-making, and their interests and values in relation to the environment being taken into account. To put the matter another way, it requires a more environmental vision of the public interest.

Promoting environmental justice thus merges into the promotion of good governance. It encompasses questions about reason and obligation, and requires reflection not only about political discourse but also about the logic of mainstream legal thought. Scholarly writings often put forward deep green visions of environmental democracy and law in which the environment is valued for its own sake. This requires quite revolutionary reform.

But there are also less radical approaches to environmental democracy. Thus, there are legal reforms that ensure that environmental law regimes incorporate public participation and are better aligned with scientific understandings of ecology. Adaptive management is an example. It grew out of management and ecology studies, and is a structured process in which the information gained through regulating is fed back into the regulatory process. In many ways, it is the logical conclusion of the need for the ongoing management of environmental problems. In the US, adaptive management has become a central feature of natural resource management in a range of contexts. In the NSWLEC, Chief Judge Preston in *Telstra Corporation Limited v Hornsby Shire Council* (2006) saw adaptive management as relevant to applying the precautionary principle:

> One means of retaining a margin for error is to implement a step-wise or adaptive management approach, whereby uncertainties are acknowledged and the area affected by the development plan, programme or project is expanded as the extent of uncertainty is reduced.

Adaptive management thus requires ongoing decision-making. It also needs to be integrated into existing administrative law structures, which is not always easy. As the US environmental law scholars, Robin Kundis Craig and J. B. Ruhl, note:

> Agencies working in good faith to follow through on the promise of adaptive management . . . have found themselves facing a public

suspicious of seemingly unbounded agency discretion and courts unaccustomed to the 'dial twiddling' of adaptive management's decision-making protocol.

This situation has led to a 'watering down' of adaptive management regimes. It also reflects the way in which the incrementalism of adaptive management is different from conventional understandings of administrative decision-making. The environmental democracy that adaptive management promotes requires legal doctrine to adapt and develop.

Another example of a legal doctrine developed to take into account a more holistic understanding of the environment can be seen in the case of *Bulga Milbrodale Progress Association Inc v Minister for Planning and Infrastructure and Warkworth Mining Limited* (2013). In the context of a full appeal on the merits, Justice Preston, in the NSWLEC, described the decision of whether to grant planning permission for the extension of a coalmine as concerning a polycentric problem that 'involves a complex network of relationships, with interacting points of influence'. He set out a process to deal with a polycentric problem: identifying the relevant matters to consider; finding facts for each matter; determining the weight to give to each matter; and finally balancing the matters to 'arrive at a managerial decision'. In the case, he considered an array of social, economic, and ecological and other impacts, and rejected the application. His decision was upheld on appeal, and in doing so the New South Wales Court of Appeal had to reconcile this polycentric approach with existing administrative law principle. Legal attention to detail was again needed.

Rights

For many the pursuit of environmental justice is about ensuring the creation and enforcement of legal rights. Rights in relation to the environment can take many forms however. As most legal systems did not historically recognize rights in relation to the environment, environmental rights have primarily been the product of legal reform in the last several decades.

At their simplest, rights in relation to the environment are created by extending already existing human rights to include environmental matters. Article 21 of the Indian Constitution states that 'No person shall be deprived of his life or personal liberty except according to a procedure established by law', and this has been interpreted by the Indian Supreme Court to include a right to a clean environment. The European Court of Human Rights has recognized that environmental risks can interfere with the 'right to respect for...private and family life' as outlined in Article 8 of the European Convention on Human Rights.

There are also examples where an explicit right to a clean environment is recognized. The preamble of the Aarhus Convention states:

> that every person has the right to live in an environment adequate to his or her health and well-being, and the duty, both individually and in association with others, to protect and improve the environment for the benefit of present and future generations.

This is only in the preamble however, and is not a freestanding right. The participation, information, and justice rights contained in the Aarhus Convention are connected to this broader aspiration.

There are also examples where nature is vested with legal rights. In 2008, Ecuador ratified their constitution—Article 71 stated that nature 'has the right to integral respect for its existence and for the maintenance and regeneration of its life cycles, structure, functions, and evolutionary processes'. To that end, Article 71 gives all 'persons, communities, peoples and nations' the power to enforce these rights.

'Slow violence' and capitalism

The demand for environmental justice is also a response to the structural inequalities of contemporary society. For some scholars and lawyers, the need for environmental justice stems from the workings of capitalism. Environmental justice, in the words of philosopher Kristin Shrader-Frechette, is about a 'more equitable distribution of environmental goods'. This returns us to Charles Kingsley's sermon about 'Human Soot' (Chapter 4)—the economic processes have led to certain groups being exposed to more harm than others. Hochschild, in her study of Tea Party voters in south-western Louisiana (Chapter 4), concluded that those who lived in this highly polluted area were 'sacrificial lambs to the entire American industrial system'. In 1992 the German thinker, Ulrich Beck, went so far as to declare the emergence of a 'risk society', in which the distribution of risks is a central political theme alongside questions concerning the distribution of wealth.

The challenge of this politics is that environmental harm is not always easy to discern, and thus outrage about it is not always forthcoming. As scholar Rob Nixon argues, many environmental problems amount to a form of 'slow violence'. As he states: '[s]tories of toxic build-up, massing greenhouse gases, and accelerated species loss due to ravaged habitats are all cataclysmic, but they are scientific convoluted cataclysms in which casualties are postponed, often for generations'.

That means such environmental harms don't garner public outrage the way other forms of violence do. Nixon points to the role that novelists and other writers play in highlighting 'slow violence'. They do this through 'testimonial protest, rhetorical inventiveness, and counter-histories'. That raises questions about how these other forms of knowledge are integrated into the legal process.

What is known as the 'environmental justice movement' first emerged in the US in light of a series of scandals concerning poor and/or racial minority communities being exposed to greater levels of pollution. Some of that exposure is obvious, as in the case of south-west Louisiana where there is a heavy concentration of industry, but exposure to pollution often occurs in more hidden ways. Take the famous scandal of Love Canal in Niagara, New York. In the 1970s, after heavy rain, chemicals seeped from the ground in a residential area. Many decades earlier waste had been dumped there, covered over, and the land sold onwards very cheaply to local government who later built houses and a school on it. Information about the risks arising from the chemical wastes became lost in this process. Similar problems, of what the sociologist Scott Frickel describes as 'lost knowledge' about what land was used for and what is on it, can be seen across the world.

Addressing the inequalities created by poor environmental quality is not easy. A first step is identifying environmental problems, but that can lead to what the sociologist Michael Edelstein calls a 'double bind'. Take, for example, the issue at the heart of the Love Canal scandal—land contaminated by toxic waste. Designating land as 'contaminated' under contaminated land legislation is an important practical tool to ensure that land is properly cleaned up and the potential health risks addressed. But legally to designate something as 'contaminated' does not result in a solution. As Edelstein states: 'The dilemma is that there is rarely a quick fix for contamination; often there is no fix at all.' Residents of the contaminated land become 'disabled' as the legal designation leads to them being in the 'complex institutional context' of different regulatory bodies. Scientific uncertainties make the development of responses difficult. The label 'contaminated' also leads to a collapse in property prices. A marginalized population becomes even more so.

Concerns over environmental inequalities arise not only within nations but between nations. Poor environmental quality is a product of the race to the bottom (Chapter 6). Countries wishing to make themselves economically competitive often have no interest in addressing tragedies of the commons. Moreover, attempts to address environmental problems such as climate change at the global level potentially lead to another set of injustices—imposing international law obligations that will have a greater impact on quality of life in developing countries than in developed countries. This is one of the reasons why in the Kyoto Protocol there was a differentiation of climate change responsibilities between developed and developing countries. Questions about environmental justice merge into questions about other types of justice. This also highlights a tension in globalization. On the one hand, the global economy has led to environmental problems and inequalities. On the other hand, global responses to environmental problems are understood as important in addressing those problems and those inequalities.

Earth jurisprudence and wild law

As the American legal scholar Jedediah Purdy notes:

> ideas about nature have been much more than rhetorical flourish or metaphysical gloss. They have deeply shaped the landscapes, economies and social practices in which we continue to live. The material world—so-called natural and so-called artificial—that we inhabit is in many ways a memorial to a long running legacy of contested ideas about nature.

Much in this book has illustrated this point. Legal orders have developed with humans and their rights as their focus. Nature has been pushed to one side. For some scholars and lawyers, environmental justice thus requires a more radical ecocentric rethinking of the nature of law. It is not just a case of embracing environmental democracy, but also embracing an ecologically grounded form of law.

That rethinking can be seen in the work of Thomas Berry on 'Earth jurisprudence' and Cormac Cullinan on 'wild law'. Their associated ideas start from the observation that the wider environment brings life into being and that existence on Earth depends on the integrity of the natural environment. This they understand as diverging from conventional legal theory, and the issue is not just that the natural environment has no legal recognition, but that the ecological laws of nature are not accommodated.

Cullinan, for example, identifies two types of jurisprudence. The first is a 'great jurisprudence' which is 'manifest in the universe itself', and which is 'neither right nor wrong, and … is inherent in all things by virtue of the fact that they are part of the universal whole'. The second is an 'Earth jurisprudence', which is a set of legal theories 'to a large extent derived from, and consistent with', this great jurisprudence.

This approach may sound radical, but as some scholars have pointed out it is a conception of law that mirrors ideas of natural law in the way in which law is understood as related to a set of meta-norms. Other scholars in this field disagree about the helpfulness of this analogy. That disagreement reflects the fact that wild law is not just a tool for environmental protection but a theory of law and society.

Indigenous concepts of environmental protection

Emerging indigenous approaches to environmental protection are a paradigm of how understandings of law, society, and the natural environment can be reconfigured. New Zealand is a good example in this regard. As we saw in Chapter 6, Maori ideas are influential in New Zealand environmental law.

Concepts that are the building blocks of Western legal thought are imagined quite differently in Maori thought. The anthropologist

Marama Muru-Lanning, in her study of the different discourses of ownership in relation to the Waikato River in New Zealand, states:

> On the one hand, there is the orthodox [Western] understanding of legal ownership, whereby the river would become the exclusive ownership of individuals or groups. On the other hand, Māori tikanga understandings are less about people's exclusive ownership of a natural resource and more about their relationship with their river, and the fact that they belong to the river.

These different ideas of ownership are embodied in a deed of settlement that created a co-governance structure in 2009.

In 2014 the Whanganui River Deed of Settlement was also signed between the New Zealand government and local Maori population. It requires the river to be recognized as 'an indivisible living whole' that has 'all the corresponding rights, duties and liabilities of a legal person'. It also requires the legislative recognition of a set of intrinsic values: that the river is 'a spiritual and physical entity that supports and sustains'; that as an indivisible whole it includes 'from the mountains to the sea, incorporating the Whanganui River and all of its physical and metaphysical elements'; that Maori communities 'have an inalienable interconnection with, and responsibility to' the river; and that it is 'a singular entity composed of many elements and communities, working collaboratively to the common purpose of the health and wellbeing'. In 2017, legislation was passed through the New Zealand legislature in line with these principles.

The reality of environmental justice

As this legislation has now passed and come into operation it will, like all law, give rise to ambiguities and questions in need of adjudication. There will be a body of case law and legal practice that develops which is grounded in robust legal reasoning and a commitment to ideals of the rule of law. This legislation will thus become part of the law of the land. Law will evolve, but in doing so it will remain committed to ideas of stability and justice. It will also be an example of what Karl Llewellyn once noted, that 'without the concrete instances the general proposition is baggage, impediments, stuff about the feet'.

Environmental justice means different things to different people, and it is not a panacea for the troubles of environmental law. The disagreements and conflicts discussed throughout this book do not disappear with a commitment to environmental justice. It is not delivered by a single court case, but by the steady and ongoing management of environmental problems in accordance with principles of legitimate governance.

Environmental justice is also realized in the day-to-day practice of the law in different places. It is in many ways a humble and modest enterprise. One of my favourite photos (Figure 10) of environmental justice in action is of successful litigants celebrating outside the NSWLEC in Sydney in 2011.

The judicial case they won was not a case with a global profile. The people in the picture are not famous people. The case concerned a challenge by local residents, the 'Friends of Turramurra', to a government plan that would allow the building of high-rise residential developments in suburban areas of Sydney where there had been none. The court concluded in a carefully reasoned, 283-paragraph judgment that there were legal flaws in the decision-making process, specifically in relation to the public consultation process. The joy of the residents is not because they stopped the development (the plan was revised and consulted on again), but because the judgment required the government decision-maker to follow proper procedure and to consult with the public. The environmental justice success of the judgment was

10. Litigants celebrating their success outside the New South Wales Land and Environment Court, Sydney, Australia.

not a particular outcome, but the maintenance of the rule of law. The photo is a reminder that this is a process embedded in law and legal practice: one of the residents holds a large set of legal files and there is the pun in the sign for the coffee shop in the background. Environmental justice is not just an aspiration. It is something very real that requires attention to legal detail to bring into being.

Chapter 10
Lessons

The American legal scholar, Carol Rose, has noted that 'mature environmental law' is 'not pretty. It is past the stage of grand theory and well into the stage of acronyms and statutory sections.' This book is proof of this. My journey along the songlines of environmental law has not resulted in a simple story. There is little here that can be summed up in a single idea or written down as a bullet point list. My journey does, however, yield lessons. Those lessons are particularly important to reflect on given the era we live in.

As Anna Lowenhaupt Tsing notes, precarity is the 'condition of our times'. It is the 'condition of being vulnerable to others. Unpredictable encounters transform us; we are not in control.' That precarity takes many economic and social forms. The environmental problems of the Anthropocene are in many ways the ultimate example of that precarity. They are products of our interconnectedness. Environmental problems remind us that what we do inevitably affects the environmental quality of others.

The persistent state of precarity has not led, however, to a widespread debate about how to foster more sustainable societies that live within their ecological limits. Quite the opposite. What has emerged are populist political discourses, particularly in the US and the UK, which promise control and a nostalgic return to times when things appeared less complex. There is very little in these discourses about the finite capacity of the natural environment. 'Make America Great Again' does not allude to the need to ensure environmental quality. Rather, environmental law has been challenged as shackling freedom and free markets. The post-truth strands of these new discourses often have environmental problems as their target. Denying that an environmental problem exists is an easy way of undercutting the need for an environmental law.

In these difficult times, it is important to understand what environmental law is in all its messy intricacy. This ensures that societies know why environmental law exists and what it can do. In this regard, the journey in this book provides three lessons.

Environmental law is necessary

Collective problems require authoritative collective responses. That is the lesson of the tragedy of the commons. Most environmental problems are too large-scale, complex, and controversial to be managed through individuals negotiating with each other. Even the parking in a few streets of East Oxford needed a collective response. At one point, before regulation was introduced, residents took to posting polite notes on cars that were obviously dangerously and illegally parked, but found they had no effect.

None of this is easy. The legal and political troubles of environmental law are struggles in recharting our understandings of the physical and social world, and the relationship of law and politics to them. They are struggles about making problems visible that were previously invisible (even if they were staring societies in the face), and developing a robust set of laws to address them. It is also the case that even if an environmental law regime is developed to respond to a problem, there is always the possibility that it will be rolled back or sidelined, particularly if there is a change in political temper. This is what is occurring in the US as I write. Environmental law is necessary, but the recognition of that fact can never be taken as a given.

To stress the necessity of environmental law is not to prescribe what form it should take. Given the diversity of environmental problems, collective responses can take many forms. They can operate at all levels of government and involve the creation of different legal rights, obligations, and processes. To address complex environmental problems, environmental laws must also address issues of justice, democracy, accountability, and effectiveness. In so doing, existing bodies of law must be confronted and reflected upon.

No magic wands

Environmental law is not a set of magic wands for the troubles of environmental problems. It is not the wedding at the end of a fairy tale. The enactment of a law is not 'a happy ever after' ending. Environmental problems are rarely solved once and for all. Unfortunately, as Rebecca Solnit notes, activists often have a 'mechanistic view of change' and expect 'finality, definitiveness, straightforward cause-and-effect relationships, instant returns'. That is not the case in relation to environmental problems.

The story of environmental law is a story about the need to develop ongoing responses to environmental problems. Take parking in East Oxford. Life in my street is very different from what it was eight years ago. There are places for residents to park. It is quieter. It is safer. The environmental quality is much improved. A problem does remain however—the street still has fewer parking places than there are houses, and yet each house has the right to two parking permits. There are more and more cars parking in the street each year. As with many environmental law regimes, there will come a point where the regime will need to be reviewed, and perhaps revised so as to ensure it manages parking effectively.

Environmental law is complex. It is, and will always be, a dense body of rules, principles, ideals, and concepts. It is shaped by legal cultures. It operates on the basis of a commitment to the rule of law and ideas of legal stability. It requires reflection on existing legal ideas and concepts. It is not a simple tool for solving environmental issues, but a vast field of practice concerned with the legitimate management of environmental problems and the resolution of disputes that arise in relation to those problems.

The need for imagination

All this means that imagination matters. In *The Silo Effect*, the financial journalist, Gillian Tett, tells the story of the queen visiting the London School of Economics and Political Science in 2008. It was the year after the global crash and she asked: 'Why did nobody see the financial crisis coming?' A year later a group of economists wrote her a letter which concluded that the crisis was 'a failure of the collective imagination of many bright people'. In particular, economists focused on the refinement of particular financial models at the expense of seeing a bigger picture unfolding in the US subprime mortgage market.

The consequences of the historic failure of the collective imagination of lawyers have been less dramatic, but perhaps more significant in the long term. Legal orders did not evolve with environmental problems as their focus, and the development of environmental law has required a confrontation with this fact. This is not to say that existing governing and legal structures are rejected wholesale and destroyed. Rather, readjustment is a process of evolutionary disruption in which there is an ongoing commitment to ideas of the rule of law and legal stability. There is an inherent tension in that process between continuity and change—and it is in reconciling that tension that legal imagination has a significant role to play.

References and further reading

Below is a list of references for quotes and other material. These are listed in order of appearance and are also good sources of further reading.

Chapter 1: Troubles

Joshua Jelly-Schapiro, 'All Over the Map: A Revolution in Cartography' *Harpers Magazine* (September 2012) 75, 80, 78.
Bruce Chatwin, *The Songlines* (London: Picador, 1987) 16–17.

Chapter 2: Environmental problems

Garrett Hardin, 'The Tragedy of the Commons' (1968) 162 *Science* 1243–8.
W. J. Jackson and others, *Australia State of the Environment 2016: Overview* (Canberra: Independent Report to the Australian Government Minister for the Environment and Energy, Australian Government Department of the Environment and Energy, 2016), <https://soe.environment.gov.au>.
The work of the Intergovernmental Panel on Climate Change can be found at <http://www.ipcc.ch>.
Urgenda Foundation v The Netherlands (24 June 2015), ECLI:NL:2015:7196, para. 4.65.
Anna Lowenhaupt Tsing, 'The Global Situation' (2000) 15 *Cultural Anthropology* 327, 330.
Rebecca Solnit, *The Encyclopedia of Trouble and Spaciousness* (San Antonio: Trinity University Press, 2014) 1.

Tim Winton, *Island Home: A Landscape Memoir* (London: Picador, 2016) 161, 13.

On environmental politics generally, see Andrew Dobson, *Environmental Politics: A Very Short Introduction* (Oxford: Oxford University Press, 2016).

George Marshall, *Don't Even Think About It: Why Our Brains Are Wired to Ignore Climate Change* (London: Bloomsbury, 2014) 227.

Arundhati Roy, *The End of Imagination* (Chicago: Haymarket Books, 2016) 111.

Naomi Klein, *This Changes Everything: Capitalism v Climate* (London: Penguin 2014) 18.

Elinor Ostrom, *Governing the Commons: The Evolution of Institutions for Collective Action* (Cambridge: Cambridge University Press, 1990).

Chapter 3: The substance of environmental law

Elinor Ostrom, *Governing the Commons: The Evolution of Institutions for Collective Action* 14.

Peter Birks, 'Adjudication and Interpretation in the Common Law: A Century of Change' (1994) 14 *Legal Studies* 156–79, 158.

United Nations Framework Convention on Climate Change 1771 UNTS 107 (1992).

Convention on Biodiversity 1760 UNTS 79 (1992).

The Environmental Permitting (England and Wales) Regulations 2010 SI 675/2010.

Directive 2000/60/EC of the European Parliament and of the Council of 23 October 2000 establishing a framework for Community action in the field of water policy [2000] OJ L327/1.

Ecologically Sustainable Development Steering Committee, *National Strategy for Ecologically Sustainable Development* (Canberra: Australian Government, 1992).

Department of Communities and Local Government, *National Planning Policy Framework* (27 March 2012), <https://www.gov.uk/government/publications/national-planning-policy-framework-2>.

For an overview of US environmental law, see Richard Lazarus, *The Making of Environmental Law* (Chicago: University of Chicago Press, 2004).

Karl Llewellyn, *The Bramble Bush* (New York: Oxford University Press, 2008) 5.

Jeremy Waldron, *The Rule of Law and the Measure of Property* (Cambridge: Cambridge University Press, 2012) 53.

Bruno Latour, *The Making of Law: An Ethnography of the Conseil d'Etat* (Cambridge: Polity Press, 2010) 242–3.

Jeremy Waldron, *The Dignity of Legislation* (Cambridge: Cambridge University Press, 1999) 10–11.

For a detailed discussion of UK and EU nature conservation and waste law, see Elizabeth Fisher, Bettina Lange, and Eloise Scotford, *Environment Law: Text, Cases and Materials* (Oxford: Oxford University Press, 2013) chapters 20 and 16.

National Parks and Access to the Countryside Act 1949 (UK) s 5.

National Parks and Wildlife Act 1974 (NSW) s 5.

Act to Improve the Administration of the National Park System (General Authorities Act) 1970 54 USC §100101(b)(1)(B).

US Clean Air Act 1970 42 USC §7409.

Directive 2008/98/EC of the European Parliament and of the Council of 19 November 2008 on waste and repealing certain Directives [2008] OJ L312/3.

Oss Group Ltd, R (on the application of) v Environment Agency [2007] EWCA Civ 611 per Carnwath LJ, para. 55.

Massachusetts v EPA 549 US 497 (2007) 529, 557.

David Markell and J. B. Ruhl, 'An Empirical Assessment of Climate Change in the Courts: A New Jurisprudence or Business as Usual?' (2012) 64 *University of Florida Law Review* 15–86, 69.

Information about the conference can be found at <http://www.kcl. ac.uk/law/newsevents/climate-courts/symposium-puts-focus-on-courts.aspx>. An example of the media response can be found at James Delingpole, 'A Supreme Court Justice and the Scary Plan to Outlaw Climate Change' *The Spectator* (10 October 2015), <https://www.spectator.co.uk/2015/10/a-supreme-court-justice-and-the-scary-plan-to-outlaw-climate-change/#>.

Amitav Ghosh, *The Great Derangement: Climate Change and the Unthinkable* (Chicago: University of Chicago Press, 2016) 137.

Chapter 4: The history of environmental law

The statistics for cholera and the quote from the *Lancet* can be found in Rose George, 'The Blue Girl: Dirt in the City' in Rosie Cox and others, *Dirt: The Filthy Reality of Everyday Life* (London: Profile Books, 2011) 143.

Edwin Chadwick, *Report on the Sanitary Condition of the Labouring Population and on The Means of Its Improvement* (London: May 1842) 85.

The *Observer* is quoted in Stephen Halliday, *The Great Stink of London: Sir John Bazalgette and the Cleansing of the Victorian Metropolis* (Stroud: The History Press, 2009) 72.

John Stuart Mill is quoted in Alain Desrosières, *The Politics of Large Numbers: A History of Statistical Reasoning* (Cambridge, MA: Harvard University Press, 1998) 170.

Charles Dickens, *Hard Times* (London: Penguin Classics, 1995) 27.

Charles Kingsley, 'Human Soot' in Francis Eliza Kingsley, *Charles Kingsley: His Letters and Memories of His Life: Volume 2* (London: Henry S. King Co., 1877) 323.

Bill McKibben, 'Foreword' in Julianne Lutz Warren, *Aldo Leopold's Odyssey* (Washington: Island Press, 2016) xi.

Henry David Thoreau, *Walden* (London: Penguin Pocket Classics, 2016) 163.

Aldo Leopold, *A Sand Country Almanac and Sketches Here and There* (London: Oxford University Press, 1949) 158.

On ideas of beauty and Ruskin, see Fiona Reynolds, *The Fight for Beauty* (London: Oneworld, 2016) 10–15.

Ebenezer Howard, *Garden Cities of Tomorrow* (London: Swan Sonnenschein & Co., 1902).

Christine Corton, *London Fog: The Biography* (Cambridge, MA: The Belknap Press of Harvard University Press, 2015).

Vaughan Lowe, *International Law* (Oxford: Clarendon Press, 2007) 5.

Daniel Bodansky, *The Art and Craft of International Environmental Law* (Cambridge, MA: Harvard University Press, 2010) 21.

Dennis Meadows and others, *The Limits of Growth: A Report for the Club of Rome's Project on the Predicament of Mankind* (London: Earth Island Ltd, 1972).

Declaration of the United Nations Conference on the Human Environment (Stockholm Declaration) 11 ILM 1416 (1972).

Paris Summit as quoted in Declaration of the Council of the European Communities and of the Representatives of the Governments of the Member States Meeting in the Council of 22 November 1973 on the Programme of Action of the European Communities on the Environment [1973] C112/1, 5.

'High level of protection' in regards to the environment, see Treaty on the Functioning of the European Union, Articles 114(3) and 191(2).

E. F. Schumacher, *Small Is Beautiful: Economics As If People Mattered* (New York: Harper & Row, 1973).

Rachel Carson, *Silent Spring* (Boston: Houghton Mifflin, 1962).

Jane Jacobs, *The Death and Life of Great American Cities* (New York: The Modern Library, 1993).

Convention of the protection of the Ozone Layer (Vienna Convention), 26 ILM 1529 (1987).

Montreal Protocol on Substances that Deplete the Ozone Layer, 26 ILM 1550 (1987).

World Commission on Environment and Development, *Our Common Future* (New York: Oxford University Press, 1990).

Rio Declaration on Environment and Development, 31 ILM 874 (1992).

Non-Legally Binding Authoritative Statement of Principles for a Global Consensus on the Management, Conservation and Sustainable Development of All Types of Forests (1992).

United Nations Division for Sustainable Development, *Agenda 21* (Rio de Janeiro: United Nations, 1992).

Convention on Access to Information, Public Participation in Decision-Making and Access to Justice in Environmental Matters (Aarhus Convention), 38 ILM 517 (1999).

On analytical opportunism, see David Michaels, *Doubt is Their Product* (New York: Oxford University Press, 2008).

Arlie Russell Hochschild, *Strangers in Their Own Land: Anger and Mourning on the American Right* (New York: The New Press, 2016) 163–4, 177, 186–7, 201, 203, 138.

Anna Lowenhaupt Tsing, *Frictions: An Ethnography of Global Connection* (Princeton: Princeton University Press, 2005) 2.

Arundhati Roy, *The End of Imagination*, chapter 21.

Mike Hulme, *Why We Disagree About Climate Change: Understanding Controversy, Inaction and Opportunity* (Cambridge: Cambridge University Press, 2009) 334.

Steve Rayner, 'Foreword' in Mike Hulme, *Why We Disagree About Climate Change: Understanding Controversy, Inaction and Opportunity* (Cambridge: Cambridge University Press, 2009) xxii.

Paul Crutzen and Eugene Stoermer, 'The "Anthropocene"' (2000) *IGBP Global Change Newsletter* (41) 17.

J. R. McNeill and Peter Engelke, *The Great Acceleration: An Environmental History of the Anthropocene Since 1945* (Cambridge, MA: Harvard University Press, 2014) 209–10.

Rebecca Solnit, *Hope in the Dark* (Edinburgh: Canongate, 2016) 128.

Yaron Ezrahi, *Imagined Democracies: Necessary Political Fictions* (New York: Cambridge University Press, 2012) 37.

Chapter 5: Expanding legal imagination

International Law Commission, *Fragmentation of International Law: Difficulties Arising from the Diversification and Expansion of International Law* (Geneva: 58th Session, 13 April 2006), 11.

Martti Koskenniemi, *The Politics of International Law* (Oxford: Hart Publishing, 2011) 337.

A chronology of developments in relation to the UNFCCC can be found at <http://unfccc.int/timeline/>.

Lavanya Rajamani, 'The 2015 Paris Agreement: Interplay Between Hard, Soft and Non-Obligations' (2016) 28 *Journal of Environmental Law* 337–58, 337.

On the interface between nuisance law and planning law/regulatory authorization in England and Wales, see *Barr v Biffa Waste Services Ltd* [2012] EWCA Civ 312 and *Coventry v Lawrence & Anor* [2014] UKSC 13.

For statutory nuisance, see Environmental Protection Act 1990 (UK) s 79.

Empress Car Co (Abertillery) Ltd v Environment Agency (formerly National Rivers Authority) [1999] 2 AC 22, 35.

'Both contrary to principle and law', see A. P. Simester and others, *Simester and Sullivan's Criminal Law: Theory and Doctrine*, 6th ed. (Oxford: Hart Publishing, 2016) 105.

For other discussions of *Empress Car*, see *R v Kennedy (No 2)* [2008] 1 AC 269, 276 and Karl Laird, 'Case Comment: Road Traffic Offences: *R. v Taylor (Jack)*' (2016) *Criminal Law Review* 366–8.

National Environmental Policy Act, 42 USC § 4321.

William Rodgers, 'The Most Creative Moments in the History of Environmental Law: The What "Whats"' (2000) *University of Illinois Law Review* 1–33, 31.

Jerry Mashaw, '"Rights" in the Federal Administrative State' (1983) 92 *Yale Law Journal* 1129–73, 1129.

On 'setting the law ablaze', see Harold Leventhal, 'Environmental Decision-Making and the Role of the Courts' (1974) 122 *University of Pennsylvania Law Review* 509–55.

For an overview of EIA case law see Robin Kundis Craig, *Environmental Law in Context*, 4th ed. (St Paul: West Academic Publishing, 2016) chapter 2.

Christopher Stone, 'Should Trees Have Standing: Towards Legal Rights for Natural Objects' (1972) 45 *Southern California Law Review* 450–501.

Sierra Club v Morton 405 US 727, 734, 740, 755–6, 741 (1972).

Christopher Stone, *Should Trees Have Standing? Law, Morality and the Environment*, 3rd ed. (New York: Oxford University Press, 2010) xi.

Walton v Scottish Ministers [2012] UKSC 44, para. 152.

Chapter 6: The significance of nation states

Benedict Anderson, *Imagined Communities: Reflections on the Origin and Spread of Nationalism*, revised ed. (London: Verso, 1991) 7.

William Twining, *General Jurisprudence: Understanding Law from a Global Perspective* (Cambridge: Cambridge University Press, 2009) 10.

On legal culture, see David Nelken, 'Using the Concept of Legal Culture' (2004) 29 *Australian Journal of Legal Philosophy* 1–26.

On the Tasmanian Dams case, see *Commonwealth v Tasmania* (1983) 158 CLR 1.

On the English judicial palate, see Michael Beloff, 'Judicial Review 2001: A Prophetic Odyssey' (1995) 58 *Modern Law Review* 143–59, 153.

Vellore Citizens Welfare Forum v Union of India AIR 1996 SC 2715.

Rapanos v United States 547 US 715, 720, 811 (2006).

Phoebe Okowa, *State Responsibility for Transboundary Air Pollution in International Law* (Oxford: Oxford University Press, 2000) 65.

Tseming Yang and Robert Percival, 'The Emergence of Global Environmental Law' (2009) 36 *Ecology Law Quarterly* 615–64.

On transnational environmental law, see Elizabeth Fisher, 'The Rise of Transnational Environmental Law and the Expertise of Environmental Lawyers' (2012) 1 *Transnational Environmental Law* 43–52.

Eloise Scotford, *Environmental Principles and the Evolution of Environmental Law* (Oxford: Hart, 2017) 2.

Chapter 7: Power and accountability in environmental law

Robyn Eckersley, *The Green State: Rethinking Democracy and Sovereignty* (Cambridge, MA: MIT Press, 2004) 12, 13.

Amitav Ghosh, *The Great Derangement: Climate Change and the Unthinkable*, 136.

For an example of reporting on EU laws on kettles and toasters, see Matthew Holehouse, 'EU to Launch Kettle and Toaster Crackdown After Brexit Vote' *Telegraph* (11 May 2016), <http://www.telegraph.co.uk/news/2016/05/10/eu-to-launch-kettle-and-toaster-crack-down-after-brexit-vote2/> and European Commission, 'EC has Not Decided to Regulate Toasters or Kettles—and Could Not Decide Alone Anyway' *Euromyths Blog* (13 May 2016), <http://blogs.ec.europa.eu/ECintheUK/ec-has-not-decided-to-regulate-toasters-and-kettles-and-could-not-decide-alone-anyway/>.

Mary Douglas and Aaron Wildavsky, *Risk and Culture: An Essay on the Selection of Technological and Environmental Dangers* (Berkeley: University of California Press, 1983) 36.

Anne Davies, *Accountability: A Public Law Analysis of Government by Contract* (Oxford: Oxford University Press, 2001) 73.

Bruno Latour, *The Making of Law: An Ethnography of the Conseil d'Etat* 243.

For an example of a Fifth Amendment case in the environmental law context, see *Lucas v South Carolina Coastal Council* 505 US 1003 (1992).

Sheila Jasanoff, *The Fifth Branch: Science Advisers as Policy Makers* (Cambridge, MA: Harvard University Press, 1990) 77.

Theodore Porter, *Trust in Numbers: The Pursuit of Objectivity in Science and Public Life* (Princeton: Princeton University Press, 1995) 8.

Sheila Jasanoff, 'Epistemic Subsidiarity: Coexistence, Cosmopolitanism, Constitutionalism' (2013) 4 *European Journal of Risk Regulation* 133–41, 140.

On the precautionary principle, see Poul Harremoës and others (eds), *The Precautionary Principle in the 20th Century: Late Lessons From Early Warnings* (London: Earthscan, 2002).

Mott, R (on the application of) v Environment Agency [2016] EWCA Civ 564, para. 64.

Environmental Protection Agency v EME Homer City Generation 134 S Ct 1584, 1593–4, 1607, 1611, 1615 (2014).

Environmental Defence Society Incorporated v The New Zealand King Salmon Company Ltd [2014] NZSC 38, para. 131.

Louis Jaffe, *Judicial Control of Administrative Action* (Boston: Little, Brown & Co., 1965) 323.

Chapter 8: Ensuring the effectiveness of environmental law

Jürgen Habermas, *Communication and the Evolution of Society* (Cambridge: Polity Press, 1984) 178–9.

Tennessee Valley Authority v Hill 437 US 153 (1978).

Ronald Dworkin, *Law's Empire* (London: Fontana Press, 1986) 21.

Richard Epstein, *The Classic Liberal Constitution: The Uncertain Quest for Limited Government* (Cambridge, MA: Harvard University Press, 2014) 355.

For a recent overview of the literature on the positive interrelationship between environmental regulation and the economy, see Antoine Dechezleprêtre and Misato Sato, *The Impacts of Environmental Regulations on Competitiveness: Policy Brief* (London: Grantham Research Institute on Climate Change and the Environment, 2014).

European Commission, *Report from the Commission Monitoring the Application of European Union Law: 2015 Annual Report*, COM(2016)463 final, 5.

Carolyn Abbot, *Enforcing Pollution Control Regulation: Strengthening Sanctions and Improving Deterrence* (Oxford: Hart, 2009) 4.

On prosecution as a last resort, see Keith Hawkins, *Environment and Enforcement: Regulation and the Social Definition of Pollution* (Oxford: Oxford University Press, 1984).

Environment Agency, *Enforcement and Sanctions Statement* (Policy 1429_10 (previously EAS/8001/1/1), Version 3, 2014) 5.

Sherry Arnstein, 'A Ladder of Citizen Participation' (1969) 35 *Journal of the American Planning Association* 216–24.

Ardagh Glass Ltd, R (on the application of) v Chester City Council [2010] EWCA Civ 172.

Berkeley v Secretary of State for the Environment [2001] 2 AC 603, 615.

Eric Orts, 'Reflexive Environmental Law' (1995) 89 *Northwestern University Law Review* 1227–340.

Carol Rose, 'Rethinking Environmental Controls: Management Strategies for Common Resources' (1991) 40 *Duke Law Journal* 1–38, 9.

For a discussion of the English and Welsh contaminated land regime, see Elizabeth Fisher, Bettina Lange, and Eloise Scotford, *Environment Law: Text, Cases and Materials*, chapter 19.

Ian Ayres and John Braithwaite, *Responsive Regulation: Transcending the Deregulation Debate* (New York: Oxford University Press, 1992).

Directive 2004/35/CE of the European Parliament and of the Council of 21 April 2004 on environmental liability with regard to the

prevention and remedying of environmental damage [2004] OJ
L143/56.

Sanja Bogojević, *Emission Trading Schemes: Markets, States and Law*
(Oxford: Hart Publishing, 2013).

The 2015 UK Supreme Court decision on the EU Air Quality Directive
is *ClientEarth, R (on the application of) v Secretary of State for the
Environment, Food and Rural Affairs* [2015] UKSC 28.

Ricardo Luis Lorenzetti, 'Complex Judicial Remedies in
Environmental Litigation: The Argentine Experience' (2017) 29
Journal of Environmental Law 1–17, 17.

Chapter 9: The many forms of environmental justice

On the United Nations' 'environmental rule of law' programme, see
<http://web.unep.org/environmentalgovernance/erl/>.

On legal costs rules in England and Wales, see Civil Procedure Rules,
r 45.41.

On specialized environmental courts, see George Pring and Catherine
Pring, *Greening Justice: Creating and Improving Environmental
Courts and Tribunals* (Washington, DC: The Access Initiative, 2009).

Telstra Corporation Limited v Hornsby Shire Council [2006]
NSWLEC 133, para. 163.

Robin Kundis Craig and J. B. Ruhl, 'Designing Administrative Law for
Adaptive Management' (2014) 67 *Vanderbilt Law Review* 1–87, 10.

*Bulga Milbrodale Progress Association Inc v Minister for Planning
and Infrastructure and Warkworth Mining Limited* [2013]
NSWLEC 48, para. 31.

Kristin Shrader-Frechette, *Environmental Justice: Creating Equality,
Reclaiming Democracy* (New York: Oxford University Press,
2002) 6.

Ulrich Beck, *Risk Society: Towards a New Modernity* (Cambridge:
Polity Press, 1992).

Rob Nixon, *Slow Violence and the Environmentalism of the Poor*
(Cambridge, MA: Harvard University Press, 2011) 3.

Scott Frickel, 'On Missing New Orleans: Lost Knowledge and
Knowledge Gaps in Urban Hazardscape' (2008) 13 *Environmental
History* 643–50.

Michael Edelstein, *Contaminated Communities: Coping with
Residential Toxic Exposure*, 2nd ed. (Boulder: Westview Press,
2004) 161–2.

Jedediah Purdy, *After Nature: A Politics for the Anthropocene* (Cambridge, MA: Harvard University Press, 2015) 21–2.

Cormac Cullinan, *Wild Law: A Manifesto for Earth Justice*, 2nd ed. (Totnes: Green Books, 2011) 78.

Michelle Maloney and Peter Burdon (eds), *Wild Law—In Practice* (Abingdon: Routledge, 2014).

Marama Muru-Lanning, *Tupu Awa: People and the Politics of the Waikato River* (Auckland: Auckland University Press, 2016) 181.

For the Whanganui Iwi (Whanganui River) Deed of Settlement, see <https://www.govt.nz/treaty-settlement-documents/whanganui-iwi/whanganui-iwi-whanganui-river-deed-of-settlement-summary-5-aug-2014/>.

Karl Llewellyn, *The Bramble Bush*, 4.

Friends of Turramurra Inc. v Minister for Planning [2011] NSWLEC 128.

Chapter 10: Lessons

Carol Rose, 'Environmental Law Grows Up (More Or Less) and What Science Can Do to Help' (2005) 9 *Lewis and Clark Law Review* 273–94, 292.

Anna Lowenhaupt Tsing, *The Mushroom at the End of the World: On the Possibility of Life in Capitalist Ruins* (Princeton: Princeton University Press, 2015) 20.

Rebecca Solnit, *Hope in the Dark*, 60.

Gillian Tett, *The Silo Effect* (London: Little, Brown, 2015) 108–9, 131.

Index

SOCIAL MEDIA
Very Short Introduction

Join our community

www.oup.com/vsi

- Join us online at the official Very Short Introductions **Facebook** page.
- Access the thoughts and musings of our authors with our online **blog**.
- Sign up for our monthly **e-newsletter** to receive information on all new titles publishing that month.
- Browse the full range of Very Short Introductions online.
- Read **extracts** from the Introductions for free.
- If you are a teacher or lecturer you can order inspection copies quickly and simply via our website.